New York on $5 a Day

Also by Ardyth Kennelly

*The Peaceable Kingdom* (1949)
*The Spur* (1951)
*Good Morning, Young Lady* (1953)
*Up Home* (1955)
*Marry Me, Carry Me* (1956)
*Variation West* (2014)
*Bodies Adjacent: Ardyth's Memoir & Egon's Journal* (2023)

# New York on $5 a Day

*A Novelist's Memoir, 1963–64*

Ardyth Kennelly

SUNNYCROFT
BOOKS

PORTLAND, ORE.

*Cover art by Michael Massee*

Publisher's Cataloging-in-Publication Data
provided by Five Rainbows Cataloging Services

Names: Kennelly, Ardyth, author.
Title: New York on $5 a day : a novelist's memoir, 1963-64 / Ardyth Kennelly.
Description: Portland, OR : Sunnycroft Books, 2024. | Includes index.
Identifiers: LCCN 2024945879 (print) | ISBN 978-0-9904320-4-3 (paperback) | ISBN 978-0-9904320-5-0 (ebook)
Subjects: LCSH: Novelists, American--20th century--Biography. | New York Metropolitan Area. | Leek, Sybil. | Women--Autobiography. | Autobiography. | BISAC: BIOGRAPHY & AUTOBIOGRAPHY / Women. | BIOGRAPHY & AUTOBIOGRAPHY / Literary Figures. | BIOGRAPHY & AUTOBIOGRAPHY / Memoirs.
Classification: LCC PS3562.E55 N49 2024 (print) | LCC PS3562.E55 (ebook) | DDC 814/.54--dc23.

Library of Congress Control Number: 2024945879

Sunnycroft Books
4110 SE Hawthorne Blvd. #749
Portland, Oregon 97214
www.sunnycroftbooks.com

# Contents

# Preface

Ardyth Matilda Kennelly (1912–2005) was the author of five historical novels published between 1949 and 1956, including two best-selling Literary Guild selections. In later life, she wrote an epic literary-historical novel centered on four generations of a family in Salt Lake City (*Variation West*, published in 2014); and a poignant memoir of her life with her husband, the Viennese émigré Egon V. Ullman (*Bodies Adjacent*, 2023). *New York on $5 a Day*, a brief but charming memoir of her 1963–64 sojourn in New York City, was her last book. It's a chatty and engaging reminiscence about the unusual people she met in New York—including the English witch Sybil Leek, the writer Anzia Yezierska, the minor poet Sanders Russell, the Spanish Civil War veteran Robert Raven, and the dancer Raymond Duncan. Ardyth also writes thoughtfully and vividly about the world of New York as she herself—a well-read but not terribly worldly woman from the West—experienced it.

Ardyth's roots were in Salt Lake City, but she was born in tiny Glenada, Oregon, on the Siuslaw River near Florence. Her parents, James D. Kennelly and Lulu "Lula" Olsen, returned to Utah when Ardyth was three years old. She grew up in Salt Lake City and Albany, Oregon; and except for the years 1963–64 in New York and 1969–72 in rural Polk County, Oregon, she lived the rest of her life in Portland.

Ardyth began publishing poems and short stories at age fifteen. She gained national fame with her first novel, *The Peaceable Kingdom* (1949), which was based on the life of her maternal grandmother, a second wife in polygamy in late-nineteenth-century Utah. In the following decade, she also published *The Spur* (1951), a fictionalized account of the last days of John Wilkes Booth; *Good Morning, Young Lady* (1953), with a young heroine who meets the outlaw Butch Cassidy; *Up Home* (1955), a sequel to *The Peaceable Kingdom*; and *Marry Me,*

*Carry Me* (1956), with events based probably on the early years of her parents' marriage.

These were the books for which she was known when, a year after her husband's sudden death in February 1962, she moved to New York City to continue her writing career. But she did not find a publisher for her new books, and she returned to Portland in late 1964 or very early 1965. She developed a successful second career in the 1990s as a collage and mixed-media artist. Yet even when stricken with partial blindness late in life, she never stopped writing. As her husband wrote in his journal on Christmas Day 1947, "Her life is one of devotion to writing, so true and so sincere as to admit no doubt, ever."

\* \* \* \* \*

Ardyth wrote this memoir by hand, in two lined steno notebooks, over a mere three weeks in early 2001—at the age of 89, when she was already partly blind. She revised it only once, on a typed copy, and seems to have written the book perhaps wholly from memory. With thirty-seven years intervening, some of those memories were not quite right. I made some silent corrections of ascertainable facts in the text and added endnotes with further corrections and context.

Several of the letters and cards that Ardyth wrote from New York to her Portland literary friend Frederic "Freddy" Jacobson have survived and are included here. They provide some additional colorful details about Ardyth's experiences in New York.

\* \* \* \* \*

I want to express my gratitude to Ardyth's sister Marion Kennelly Brownell (1915–2011) for preserving Ardyth's manuscripts and for sharing many memories with me; and to Marion's children—Michael Massee, Timothy J. Pettibone, and Ardyth L. Morehouse—for their continuing support in the publication of the late-life work of their uniquely talented aunt.

Nancy Trotic
Sunnycroft Books
October 2024

New York on $5 a Day

⟋  ⟋  ⟋

WE WERE ACQUAINTED, I was living there at the time, and so when she was hired by CBS to appear on their hit Wednesday night show, she wrote and asked if I would like to meet her at the airport in New York and I said I would. My nephew and his wife, temporary New Yorkers trying to get on the stage, were quite thrilled about it when they found out who Sybil was. That was this acquaintance's name, Sybil Leek, and for pride's sake I said *she* had got in touch with *me* rather than that I had read this little piece about her in our Portland, Oregon, Sunday paper, when all kinds of little news items get in, and thought about it awhile and then decided to get in touch, because she was a witch with a coven (as well as having a small antique shop), one of the first witches to surface in the 1960s. A good witch, of course, with a lot of Welsh lore she had researched for the BBC, she said, about how to cast spells and draw down the moon and such as that, and straighten out whatever was wrong with anyone's life.

The main thing wrong with mine, besides my being a bereft widow for about a year, was the same thing that had been wrong since 1956, when my fifth and last book came out. Now it was 1963. And I wanted to be able to write a best-seller, I am sorry to say, and have more money than the $300 a month my husband had arranged, bless his darling heart, for me to have if ever he should be gone. Not from my endeavors, for what I got from the books I always looked on as fairy money. In fact, as I had gone through the Depression, *all* money was fairy money to me. From my books, two of them having been Literary Guild book club selections, there had been enough to give us quite a bit of leeway. Not like today, when people like Martin Amis and Hillary Clinton make $8 million on a book, but considerable leeway, which I didn't have anymore, for fairy money is like dew, gone before you know it. And when prices go up, even if very gradually, even *real* money, such as a person's income consists of, becomes volatile.

So it occurred to me that if I could sit down and write a nice book, the fairy money would start coming in again and "all manner of thing would be well," as that medieval woman said.

WHEN I WROTE SYBIL, I told her about needing to have a spell cast so I could write again like a professional author. Actually, I was getting quite scared, what had happened to me being so much like what had happened to a lovely writer named Katharine Brush. She had written a famous book called *Young Man of Manhattan* and another famous book or two and had had all kinds of articles written about her and lots of pictures taken of where she lived, what she wore, and the renowned people she mixed with. One article stuck in my mind, about how she had bought an extra floor in her apartment house so she could have this wonderful office built with these gorgeous windows so she could see all over, and a big round desk and lots of space to walk up and down in, thinking, and how she had this rose-colored typewriter and the *Encyclopedia Britannica* and the *Oxford English Dictionary* and a maid to bring coffee and everything her little heart could think of. And she would write from 10 until 3 every day, five days a week.

When I read about Katharine Brush was when I was getting up every morning "without one thought of harm or wrong" and writing my second or third book, so I was very interested. But then the articles about Katharine Brush kind of dwindled away, and the pictures. And quite a long time after that, I read that she couldn't stand her wonderful custom-made office, it made her sick to her stomach to go into it, and she had rented a dingy little room with nothing in it but an old office desk and her old black typewriter. And I don't know if this is true or if I just imagine it, but that was the end of Katharine Brush. No more books. And then she must have died in all her wit and glory.

Then I started getting what I would call quite leery myself, because a studio, as we called such places in those days, that in my idleness I had had built in the attic of our house in Portland, with a skylight and a suit of lights hung on the wall and a round sophisticated desk, didn't work for me any more than Katharine Brush's had for her. Instead of turning out book number six, the new typewriter acted up like a balky horse. Then fresh air didn't flow in and out of the room anymore, and the dye in the carpeting started making a person sick. I didn't rent office space but just shut the door and went downstairs, never to step foot up there again. That didn't help, though.

My heart beat funny and my throat felt dry when I swallowed. And I decided that the *Oxford English Dictionary*—ten volumes, as I look back, of the entire language that conquered India and everything in its wake and is still a contender after five hundred years—millions of quotations from England's heavenly choir of literary angels so dazzling that you could sit and read and turn the pages till you died right there under big books weighing twenty pounds apiece—might be fine for the William Buckleys of this world, but for certain others was the work of the Devil. You can't just throw it away, either.

But when my husband died and I sold the house, that was my chance, out it went. Hundreds of other books, too, which I quickly tried to replace, going to book sales, second-hand and even new bookstores and buying books till hell wouldn't have them, as the saying goes. Not the great dictionary, though, and I have never seen it again.

ONE BOOK I BOUGHT was a paperback called *New York on $5 a Day*, and I went there and it was true, but not if you become a resident, which I did, renting an apartment for $115 a month on Sixteenth Street between Seventh and Eighth Avenues in The Village. (When I started writing this, I tried to get a copy, but while you can find out everything about it on the Internet—the year it came out, how many times it was reprinted, and who the smart little hard-working cookies were who wrote it—try as you will, you can no more find *New York on $5 a Day* than you can find the New York it talks about that once was, then vanished.) By that time Sybil and I were quite well acquainted.

I can't remember if she had cast any spells for me, but if so, they hadn't done any good, and I realized that a good witch might not be much more of a help than a new studio. In New York, though, I started having a few ideas. Not many. It took me quite a while to get settled, have bookcases built, and such as that. I was fifty-one years old by then, but New York carpenters, painters, the butcher, and in fact New York men in general are quite susceptible to tall women.

In *New York on $5 a Day*, I read about these two or three places in nice locations where you could get second-hand clothes. Not like you would get at the Salvation Army or St. Vincent de Paul, but nice sponged and pressed things that had supposedly belonged to the ladies in *Vogue* and *Harper's Bazaar*—Truman Capote's swans, in fact. They cost quite a bit, but well they might, coming from Paris or London or Bendel's or Saks Fifth Avenue. The problem with them, though, was that they were mostly evening wear that you would have no occasion for, although by this time I had a beau who went to the opera (but just in ordinary seats). And the second drawback was that the clothes were awfully small. But for something as beautiful as some of them were, it was easy to diet. Or if not easy, it wasn't too hard, especially if you had already bought the creation and tried it on every day until you could zip it up or button it or whatever. And I walked everywhere. In fact, I had two beaux, and the butcher brought me a fish (a pike or whatever it was) when he went on vacation. I was so surprised (it was one of those big fishes with a long sharp nose) that I hardly even said thank you, and I'm sorry for that now, forty years later.

Another thing I did was to pay $25 to learn how to put makeup on at Helena Rubinstein's. That turned out to be a good idea, though my beautiful younger sister, Scandinavian cousins and I were by no means strangers to makeup, especially mascara. But this operator at Helena Rubinstein's, with her own luxurious office and framed photographs on the wall showing her herself in a satin smock making up *Princess*

*Elizabeth*, to be crowned Queen that very day in nineteen fifty-something, was a real artist, and I felt honored to meet her. Surprises like that are what is so wonderful about New York. One day I was uptown in Times Square and I happened to notice this sign saying Foot Specialist. I walked up two flights of stairs and here was his office. So I went in and here were more photographs, but big ones this time—almost like posters—of life-size pugilists. Because this doctor was the foot specialist to several famous prizefighters, champions, whose names I can't think of now, but one of them was Sonny Liston. New Yorkers are talkers, so it was fascinating. He told me all kinds of things—that wherever the fighters had their training camps, he would go for two or three days and take care of their feet: "Feet are very important." The coming weekend he was going to Lake Placid, I think it was, where Sonny Liston had his training camp. He asked me if I would like to go with him, I might find it very interesting and a little off the beaten path. I am sure I would have, but I said no, and I'm sorry I did. As Edna St. Vincent Millay pointed out:

> *All that delightful youth forbears to spend*
> *Molestful age inherits, and the ground*
> *Will have us; therefore, while we're young, my friend—*

(Of course fifty-one wasn't that young, but nearly forty years down the line it does seem so.)

> *The Latin's vulgar, but the advice is sound.*
> *Youth, have no pity; leave no farthing here*
> *For age to invest in compromise and fear.*

So I missed out on that, as I had done and would do for a lot of my life, "missing so much and so much."

BUT IT'S ASTONISHING about New York. The first time I went to my beau's house on 110th just off of Broadway for lunch, he was cooking it and needed something from the store. I jumped up and said I would get it. He told me where to go, and in fact when I got off the bus (I didn't think at that time I knew how to use the subway, but I soon learned), I saw all these little shops with fruit and vegetables and candy and cheese and bread and wine, each in a separate shop—not like in the West, where one store sells all these things and maybe umbrellas, scales, and wheelchairs as well. It was just one thing he wanted, so I didn't need a list.

So off I went, the busy streets reminding me, as they would do the whole time I was there, of the movie *Street Scene*, and while I was standing on a corner waiting for the light to change, somebody took me by the arm and asked, "Would you please help me across the street? I'm blind." It was an old woman. "Blind and not blind." I found out what she meant later, when she told me about her degenerative eye disease, and when I grew as old as an old tree myself, had no central vision, couldn't see my face in the mirror or see lots of things, but with my glasses and a magnifying glass could still write on a lined tablet and read the newspaper and books—when I became, in short, like her, "blind and not blind"—I thought, wasn't that strange? Are there roots to coincidence? Why did she pick just me to help her across the street? Then to the bank on the corner, where we stood in line to get a check cashed, then home to where she lived, which turned out to be an apartment on 113th Street in an apartment building at the *very address* which I, three thousand miles away, had chosen at random to be where my favorite character in my last book lived.

She didn't seem like too interesting an old bent-over, white-haired lady to start with, but in the bank, when we were standing in line, she suddenly said "Ripeness is all," and I thought, well, Shakespeare, you know. So when she wanted me to walk her the three blocks home, I did, and saw where she lived. And heard she was an author who had written a couple of best-sellers in her young days but then fell silent like somebody else I knew of, which seemed coincidental indeed. I mean, we two with almost identical literary histories meeting in the midst of three or four million people rushing hither and yon. Her name was Anzia Yezierska.

I BOUGHT WHATEVER IT WAS I had been sent for, for our lunch, and rushed back to Herman's apartment. He was furious: "I didn't know what had happened. I thought you were dead!" He didn't think it was unusual at all for Anzia and me to meet, or about her address or anything. He was a nice beau, but from the first time I met him on a blind tea date arranged by a second cousin of my husband and found him tall and handsome, very bourgeois Viennese, looking like the old-time movie actor Conrad Nagel, whose looks I never could stand, I didn't think anything in particular could come of it.

He had been a lawyer in Vienna, the lawyer of this second cousin's father's nacre firm, but during the Hitler years, when he and his wife left their two college-age daughters in England till they could come to this country a year or two later, he either couldn't or just didn't open a law office, and he became a professor instead. After their children joined them and they lived happily long enough for the girls to find lovely husbands, one a musician in the Boston Symphony and the other a prosperous entrepreneur, Herman's wife died. I know just what she was like, a sweet girl of Vienna, with a sweet caroling laugh and charming manners. The daughter of a prosperous family, she knew how to dress and entertain and do everything. I'm sure that when she died, a year or so before my husband did, Herman was devastated. They went to concerts and for walks in Central Park and did everything together.

But people get over things, they have to; it's a little less easy at sixty-nine than at fifty, but they muddle through. And Herman still had their big apartment with all the nice carpets and the polished grand piano and the lovely china. And he went about, had a lady friend or two. Except for the fact that he was a Democrat, he was a born Republican, but otherwise—in appearance and every way—he was the closest thing to a nice beau that anyone could wish for.

He was very annoyed at me for not coming right back from my errand and not calling him, and he didn't seem to think my meeting Anzia was any excuse at all. But we kissed and made up and everything was cool again. He took me to see the daughter who lived closest, and when he was in the hospital with some kind of prostate problem, he asked his doctor to come to the room and meet me, and his other daughter came to visit too, so I met her. Both daughters were sweet girls of Vienna with English accents and the same caroling laughter I had heard in both women and girls from Vienna that I met in Portland before and during World War II, when quite a few Austrians settled there—Viennese, of that particular charm and historic grace.

My husband, Egon Ullman (an eye, ear, nose and throat doctor), was also from Vienna; but he had come to America to join a small clinic in Corvallis, Oregon, in 1926, when I was fourteen. But of course we didn't know each other then. I don't believe he would have liked Herman a lot, because he would have reminded him of his Cousin Hans. Hans was older and taller than Egon, and once when Hans's father, Egon's uncle, heard Egon ask his father why he couldn't have a key of his own, his uncle said, "When you get as big and as smart as your Cousin Hans, then you can have a key!" And as I say, Herman looked like Conrad Nagel and Hans, so I'm sure Egon wouldn't have liked him. I met Hans once and soon saw that as far as smartness and cuteness and style were concerned, Egon could have run rings around him. But by then it was too late to tell him. When that happens, isn't it too bad?

TO TAKE HERMAN'S MIND off my malfeasance with Anzia, I mentioned the witch who was coming to be on the CBS program I knew Herman used to watch. I said I was supposed to meet her at the airport. But he acted more put out than mollified by this information. He said sternly, "How in the world did you get acquainted with someone like that?"

I'm sorry to say I was ashamed to tell him I read about her being a witch in the paper and wrote to ask her to cast a spell for me so I could write book number six without having to wait another ten years. Herman didn't seem to realize that I—like Anzia and several other examples I had collected—wasn't really an author anymore. I think he thought I was, and could write a book for the Literary Guild anytime I wanted. "Oh, she wrote to me," I said, "because Gollancz published some of my books over there in England and she does research for the BBC or someone, and she thought maybe a feature about polygamy in Utah might be interesting." Herman wasn't too fond of the polygamy in my background, either (most of my books being about those primitive old times in the West). So he didn't look entertained by this. "Why you? Why doesn't someone from CBS meet her?" "Oh, Herman, it's going to be fun!" I thought of Robert Frost's poem — *"I'm going out to clean the pasture spring. You come, too."* "Why don't you come, too?" "To meet a *witch?*" I knew what he would say. Still, he was a nice presentable beau, and I was glad to have him.

I went in a taxi.

As NEW YORK ON $5 A DAY pointed out, you could go anywhere in New York in a taxi for not very much at all. I don't remember how much it cost to go to JFK, but I enjoyed the ride, talking to the driver about this witch friend of mine coming to be on television. He said he believed in witches. He believed in everything. Why not?

I had quite a wait, and pretty soon I noticed all these men crowded along a sort of upper balcony waiting for someone, so I decided to go up and ask who they were waiting for. Now I realize it might even have been one of the presidential candidates, for it was an election year, 1964. I feel foolish to say I didn't follow any of what was going on or even have a television set, but for some reason we on the West Coast couldn't even get television till 1954, and Egon and I, being big readers and book collectors, just didn't get with it too soon. And in New York, settling down, I didn't think that if you didn't watch television you were to all intents and purposes an illiterate. Herman, of course, and others soon saw that I didn't know what was going on as far as the world was concerned and heard how I didn't have a TV hooked up yet, but we chatted along, and all I didn't know — a very great deal indeed — didn't seem to matter.

But I was sure all these men in Frank Sinatra hats crowding along that upper balcony at the airport were reporters. So I went up and just casually edged up to a reporter towards the end of the line looking at his watch, at two closed doors ahead, then down at the crowd in the concourse below, and I ventured: "I bet I know who you're waiting for. I bet you're waiting for that witch from England."

"What?" he said crossly.

"The witch from England. With the coven." I hadn't spoken loudly, but another reporter pricked up his ears, and at that moment there was a surge in the crowd downstairs and it parted, and here came the new arrivals. Upstairs on the balcony the two doors opened, and the reporters crowded in to see whomever it was they had waited to see. All except the reporter I had spoken to and the other one who had pricked up his ears; they rushed downstairs alongside me, because here was Sybil Leek, the Sunday supplement witch from England, in purple lace stockings, with another young woman. You couldn't miss her. The two young men and a third with a camera who had joined them crowded around her, setting off flash bulbs just like in Pathé News, then before I could do anything but smile and wave at Sybil and mouth "I'm Ardyth," all three started interviewing her. That lasted a few minutes, then they rushed away, she and I embraced, and she introduced me to Louise, an unobtrusive little housewife in a yellow dress who belonged to her coven for want of something else to do and who said she had to see everything in two days, because that was as long as her husband was allowing her in America.

The one you would notice was Sybil, in her stockings and a plaid coat two sizes too small, and heads did turn. But it was more what she exuded, heat, like a parlor stove with the draft open. Her eyes looked like a horse's running in a race, and her plentiful hair seemed to lift and subside like water. "Well, here we are then." Louise went and got their luggage, just two small bags, I went and got a taxi and we went home. The visitors were supposed to stay at the Americana, a big new hotel CBS had picked out for them for three nights. This was Tuesday, the show Sybil would be on was on Wednesday. So as soon as the girls had eaten supper with me, they would go to their hotel and go to bed.

Looking back, I don't know why I would have wanted to cook supper for them. Maybe I thought it would seem more hospitable, and at that time I could put on quite a nice meal.

After Egon died, I was so sad and missed him so much—especially since I didn't have work for consolation—that I didn't know what to do. That last year, with his health worsening, had been like being lost in the Horse Latitudes. He would come home from the hospital where he worked and that was it; we read the evenings away. He was interested in the history of medicine and was making notes for a book he was going to write someday, so his reading was along those lines, while I would pick up something and follow the path of least resistance. That last year I read all of Fanny Burney and whatever came to hand of Dr. Johnson's circle, a lot of volumes of Boswell and Mrs. Thrale and that whole outfit. And was sorry for it when, after Egon was gone, a colleague of his and his wife invited me to a dinner at their house for what seemed like an awful lot of people. At dinner, I had no more idea what they were talking about than if it had been in Choctaw. *Last Year at Marienbad* was the movie of the season, and everyone was making a guess as to what it was supposed to mean. They talked about records, too, a play that had come to town, a concert, a lecture, and I sat like a half-wit, because that's what you might as well be if nothing rings a bell.

Sybil, Louise, and I didn't have any trouble talking. They liked the apartment and wanted to know all about it, how much it cost and what all I had done to fix it up, and then I wanted to know all about them, which for some unknown reason wasn't as fascinating as I would have thought it would be.

They liked my dinner, which I had taken quite a bit of trouble to prepare, setting the table beforehand and having everything ready so that, just like magic, it could be heated and served. Sybil did something that pleased me when I took a head of washed and chilled lettuce out of the icebox and began cutting it up with the butcher knife. "Oh, my heavens!" she cried, throwing up her hands in horror. "You must *never* cut up lettuce with a knife. You *tear* lettuce, *never* cut it, or you will have bad luck. But you won't," she said, "because you stopped before it was too late."

After dinner I called a taxi and they went to their hotel, hoping they could sleep and not think about Sybil being on American television the next night. But Louise said Sybil knew a spell to cast, so she was sure they would sleep. For some unknown reason, Sybil didn't seem to like this and quickly changed the subject—which I did too when they wondered where my television was (which I didn't yet have).

I called Herman the next day and told him about the witches' having arrived, about not cutting lettuce with a knife and all that had transpired. Of course he was going to watch the show? Was he going to call his daughters? "To watch, you mean?" he said. "Why would I do that?" "Oh, because of me meeting Sybil at the airport and everything," I said. "I wonder when I will cease to be amazed at American frivolity," he said. So that made me feel like I had somehow done something dumb and silly, which I often felt when talking to him.

The morning after the show, the phone rang before eight o'clock and who should it be but Sybil. "Oh, my," she said, drawing a deep sigh. "We are into it now."

"Who is?" I said. "Did anything go wrong with the show?"

"Everything," she said. "Everybody knew my secret, that I was the witch from England, because of those reporters. I was on the news Tuesday night. And it was in the papers. CBS is furious. They say they'll never ask me to be on anything again!"

"I'm so sorry!"

"Why should you be sorry? It wasn't your fault. Besides, it doesn't matter. About fifty people called after Louise and I got back to the hotel." And one of the calls, she said, was what she wanted to speak to me about now. A television station with a news show at noon wanted to interview her, and what she wondered was, could they do that in my apartment? They looked to the hotel, but it didn't seem very interesting. So they thought she might know someone—not necessarily a witch, but maybe with books like ancient lore as a background? She thought of my apartment and wondered—?

I was thrilled, even not knowing one station from another. But noon? Look how late it was already. I wouldn't have to do anything, Sybil said. They would just sit down in front of the books— Well, okay. I could set it up like they were having tea. "Somebody will pop in to discuss things. Don't worry," Sybil said. She meant beforehand, and sure enough they did. In what seemed like a few minutes, here came a big truck from a TV station that filled up narrow Sixteenth Street, then out came coils of wire and rope and cartons and I don't know what all, and several men and at least one girl with glasses and long straight hair parted in the middle began piling all this up. "At least you're on the sidewalk," a man rushing by with a big light said crossly, "that's some consolation."

"May I speak to you, Mrs. Ullman?" a woman's voice in back of me said morosely. It was Miss Berger, my landlord's secretary from upstairs. "Mr. Raven is *very upset*. Will you tell me what's going on?"

"I'll run right up and explain," I said, turning away to do that.

"No," Miss Berger said, catching my sleeve. "He wants you to tell me. The children are crying. And Mrs. Raven is upset too, as you might imagine. Two blind people! You can't raise Cain like this without permission—!"

Things got straightened out, but my landlords were very stirred up, not to have had a word said to them about their house being barricaded.

THEY SET GREAT STORE by their four-story brownstone—big enough to accommodate several apartments, great wide marble staircases, and lots of nooks and crannies—especially Mr. Raven.

"For as I understand it," the woman at the cleaner's on the corner told me, "she was the one with the money, her being related in some way to the people that own Gasner's Restaurant. They met at a Blind Society, some kind of gathering, a party or something. Sat by each other, maybe danced for all I know. It's wonderful how the blind just try to act like normal people. She was born blind, I guess, but he was just like anybody till he joined that crazy Abraham Lincoln Brigade and went to Spain to fight the innocent Catholics, what was all that about? And got injured by grenades that took out his eyes and partially crippled him, although he helped with all the remodeling they did after his in-laws bought the place. And he does their shopping and takes care of the baby and that older one better than a woman, so they tell me—"

"Lovely blue eyes," I said. "I don't know if you've seen that big portrait of him, the one that Moses Soyer did—hanging right back of him in his office—?"

"Where he sits all day when he hasn't got something else to do, with that Miss Berger, staring into space. I know, I've seen it. Mr. Raven was a very good-looking man with his real eyes and not damaged or anything," the woman from the cleaner's said. "I'll tell you something. Her being related to the Gasner's Restaurant people didn't hurt a bit. He mixed with artists and had big ideas. Well, no money worries; especially for a blind person like that, it makes a big difference. Miss Berger got the job taking in the rents and everything for the Ravens. She's very smart and sees to it he gets good renters and nothing goes wrong." I didn't mind if I went to pick up something and the cleaning hadn't quite come back from wherever the cleaners sent it out, I would just sit down and the woman there would tell me what was happening in the neighborhood.

SYBIL CAME AT A LITTLE after ten, and I sat on the staircase so she and the news people could proceed. It took quite a while for the scene to be set, and she would either talk to someone who wasn't busy or come and sit with me on the staircase. But I could see she thought it was more to her advantage to talk to them than to me. As someone who worked in broadcasting herself—so she said, she had done everything—she was shocked that I didn't have a television.

And now it was beginning to dawn on her that a really long time had passed since I had had a book published. Some people just weren't serious about work. About the world or anything, scientific advances— I was serious, I said, when we had a chance to talk. But of course what I wanted was a spell— spells—to straighten everything out, and the better I got acquainted with Sybil, the more I could see that if I expected magic from her, I was barking up the wrong tree. She was deadly in earnest. But not about witchcraft, which she seemed to have taken up like the little boy in the poem took up sneezing—"because he knows it teases." She could see it titillated, brought her attention, and it doesn't take much to hook some people on that. Her life's endeavor was to prevail, and when the witchcraft she took up like quilting seemed to help her do that by the interest it elicited, much to her astonishment, why, she was a witch, in on the ground floor. But not a learned witch, so that was why when anyone asked her a question, she would just look wise and say *hm-n.*

She never went back home. In New York she would be asked to go on the *Today Show* and the *Tonight Show*, and to cast a spell at the World's Fair, which would soon open. For that, my nephew Michael and I persuaded her to wear a witch's costume he copied from a book about Wales. Michael dabbled in anything connected to the theater and proved to be especially talented in costume design. I bought the goods and he made her a wonderful black dress, a cloak and a broad-rimmed pointed hat with a little grey velvet mouse running around the crown, tied to a string. When he tried the dress on her, he said some kind of an odor emanated from her that almost asphyxiated him. I didn't notice it, and I think it was just Michael wanting her to be a real witch, smelling like the fumes of hell.

A few years later, Sybil wrote and published a book about astrology. By that time she seemed to have forgotten all about when she came to America, how CBS had hired her to come and be a witch on *To Tell the Truth.* And how the surprise had been spoiled by someone (not mentioning any names), how I had met her and her fellow witch Louise at the JFK airport, and how for a few days she had been nearly as well known as the Wicked Witch of the West. For some reason all that had to be forgotten. Here is what she wrote in her book *Reincarnation: The Second Chance*, published by Stein & Day, New York, 1974:

> Years ago, I was particularly upset at the cir-
> cumstances that brought me to the United
> States. [. . .] I had left Europe as a well-known
> personality used to the company of people who
> had a respect for the religion I followed. In the
> United States, in the early days, I was treated
> like either a half-baked idiot or something that
> properly belonged in a freak show. [. . .] It took
> a year for me to adjust to living in the United
> States, to realize the part I had to play in the
> occult explosion there.

That part had nothing to do with Wicca, with wearing a pointed hat, or listening to petitioners wanting the moon drawn down and spells cast. These latter soon found they were wasting their breath. She was the kind of witch the attendant is at the HMO who can't run the computer. Still, her seemingly profound silences, with a wise-sounding *hm-n* now and then, and "Let me think about that" upon parting, kept her afloat through several days' guest appearances. The man who ran the *Today Show* invited her to stay at his apartment for a few days; a prominent couple did too. But people in America were so funny, she told me. She had hardly settled into these havens when unexpected things came up and the visit was over. The most unexpected seemed to be how quickly people sensed she wasn't going to solve whatever their big problem was that made them invite her in the first place. I don't know whether she cast any spells, but if she did, they didn't work; what witchcraft magic she was supposed to have brought from her home base vaporized, and quite soon she fled New York. At first she went to Hollywood to visit I think Shirley MacLaine (but I could be mistaken), who paid her way to come down and cast a spell. Or it could have been the blond actress who needed to have the horrible awful not good very bad karma dispersed that followed a murder committed by a member of her family.

At first we kept in touch, and I heard by postcard that that visit was a disaster due to the people not having a normal bone in their bodies. But then, her way paid again, she was invited to Hawaii. And it was there, apparently, that she changed horses in midstream and gave up witchcraft and being a witch, to become in due time a medium to Hans Holzer; then a Theosophist; then a "society" astrologer; then an author of books on astrology and reincarnation; then a syndicated columnist on the supernatural; and at last if not the *real* reincarnated Madame Blavatsky, at least the nearest approximation till the real thing comes along. Oh, yes, exophthalmic eyes, same bust size, gap between the two front teeth, and being able to pick out Charles Luntz in a crowded room though she had never seen him before in her life.

Eventually, many hundreds of looneytunes and others knew who she was and wrote letters to her the way I had done. Of course, success and celebrity—especially after she began lecturing about reincarnation—had their price. Disappointment early on when what CBS had paid her for her appearance ran out, the folks at home wouldn't send money to further a career here in America—especially when she wrote them that witches in America were more or less made fun of and she wanted to be something else where there was more respect—and then, as the years went on, a few actual dangers to life and limb. She felt no anger, she wrote in *Reincarnation*, even when confronted with "extreme examples of intolerance [. . .] including occasions in Connecticut, where religious fanatics stoned me (they missed!); in Minneapolis, where a poor demented religious maniac tried to stab me; and at universities where new-style Jesus freaks have tried to break up my lectures." But, she said, "I am grateful that my present incarnation gives me the opportunity to be versatile, and today I am no longer afraid to give anything up and start a new life." In other words, don't hang around to be dissed. Fly like a bird.

While she was in New York, I spoke about her to Herman several times, including how I took her to a store called Lane Bryant. (It was highly recommended by *New York on $5 a Day*, which I didn't say—in fact, I never mentioned even the *existence* of such a book to him, or anybody I met back there. But it was my guide and my salvation.)

Lane Bryant was this store where you could get larger-sized clothes that looked nice on people at truly bargain prices, so I took Sybil there and she was delighted. Especially since several people in the vicinity recognized her and said, "Didn't I see you on television?" or "Weren't you on *To Tell the Truth?*" She didn't even mind when they said, "Aren't you that *witch?*" for she hadn't decided at that time not to be a witch anymore. Mostly, Herman just said he hadn't seen her and didn't want to, but once he said quite impatiently, "Why would you be interested in such a person?"

ANZIA THOUGHT HIS ATTITUDE might be because of his friends, mostly European, and his two daughters, who certainly wouldn't want a stepmother who knew anybody peculiar in case we ever got married. I had told Anzia about him being my beau and she thought that was nice. Anzia was about eighty then, but she had a beau too, a nice young English professor who came to see her, had published an article about the books she had written and who might write her biography. I met him at her place and thought how much nicer it would be to have him for a beau than Herman. Academics all have to mark their space, and it's not so easy anymore with professors—tens of thousands now because of overpopulation, instead of just hundreds—combing through the libraries down to the deepest depths to find some author or poet or historical person, all for their own, to write about and be the expert on.

So this young English teacher had stumbled upon Anzia, about forty years past her fame, and was coming to town as often as he could to talk to her and listen and take notes for some kind of a definitive book about women or immigrants or the Polish Jews or the gifted poor. With "a tongue that ran like a squirrel in the park," Anzia was a find for him. One of her novels had been about her own big family crowded into two or three rooms on the Lower East Side and about herself and an older sister, in particular, who was very beautiful and whom Anzia could almost have killed as a consequence. That sister went on to marry the man who wrote "Happy Days Are Here Again" and live in Hollywood and have a lovely easy life, while Anzia's was nothing but toil and trouble. Not during the time she had a best-selling book and a contract to write films in Hollywood; it seemed like nothing could bother her again. But of course something could. She fell flat in Hollywood and went back home.

Her next book didn't do as well, and after a hiatus long enough to be scary, neither did another book or two, nor the articles she stooped to write. But she had a life, met other writers socially, became friends; yet nothing seemed to come of anything. Somehow she associated herself with John Dewey, of the Dewey Decimal System and immortal renown as an educator, and had, so she told me, a daughter by him. Whether he ever acknowledged the child I do not know. Louise was a very bright girl, as you would expect if John Dewey was her father, and had a lovely job in some other town. She would come to see her mother now and then, and on one of those occasions I met her—a joyous occasion for both mother and daughter, for Louise had just become engaged and was going to get married in a few months' time. Anzia, who had never married herself, was very pleased, because Louise was not especially outgoing or noticeable, and at the age of about forty, which she appeared to me to be, it seemed she might never team up with anyone. But she had, a real catch—Anzia said she could hardly believe it. About Louise's age, he was a mathematician so brilliant that he had been invited that very summer to move to Princeton for several weeks to mix with other of the world's smartest people, and by doing so between them further space travel and I don't know what all. Each scientist was to have his own house on the campus, and it was a great honor.

So Anzia was very proud, and so was Louise, who had to return to her job for the nonce until the time came to quit and get married. But the son-in-law-to-be had had a beautiful upbringing and so started to act like Anzia was his mother-in-law already, even inviting her to come to Princeton and stay with him. Anzia was so happy she didn't know what to do, and she invited her English professor to come and visit her there. She invited me, too, and gave me careful directions: "You take the subway to such and such a station, then there's a little train you get on that takes you nearly to our door." I followed orders and got right there, to a sort of bungalow with hardwood floors and a lovely fireplace.

Now comes the part I am nearly ashamed to tell. I knew it was a famous college, on the campus of which all this wonderful and prestigious stuff was happening. But to tell you the truth, I didn't realize till quite a while later that it was *Princeton* itself, so hallowed in the memories of so many beloved writers like—well, you know—and that the little rattling train I got on was *that* train immortalized by—well, I don't have to tell you. Often I have wondered how I, "missing so much and so much," made it through this far. It was bad enough anyway, but during the years I wrote my books, such as they were, I might as well have been hit on the head and put into deep freeze. I remember how surprised I was when I took my niece and some other guests to the one concert by the Beatles in Oregon during their tour of the nation in 1965. We took our seats early, and as all this rampant youth poured in, I couldn't believe my eyes at their *clothes* and *shoes*, and here were all these bales of *hair* grown while I was sleeping. Who were these people? Where had they come from? And so it has been.

The English professor, of course, could have told you chapter and verse about the university and the little rattling train. I don't know whether his book about Anzia ever came out. But years later I saw that a Louise somebody had written a book about Anzia, which I always meant to pick up but didn't.

Anzia herself wrote something while I was still in New York. It was a short article about something that happened in her apartment, where she left the window open all the time. She called me about it in great agitation not long after. What happened was that one morning a bird flew into her rooms and nearly scared her to death. Now that I am in just about the shape she was in then—with a form of blindness called macular degeneration, where your central vision is destroyed and you see by fits and starts, and you have arthritis and jumping out of a chair is almost impossible—to have a bird fly in and be panicky and swoop around would scare a person out of seven years' growth. It did Anzia, she screamed and hollered and tottered into the hallway, and a woman came to help catch the poor bird. Anzia was so afraid the woman would hurt it, which I would have been too. But she didn't, she caught it, let it fly away unharmed. Hoping she wasn't going to die of a heart attack, Anzia settled down to recover.

But "something good will come of that," as the old song says, or come of almost anything if you wait long enough. And something did in this case, for after years of writer's paralysis, Anzia wrote a story about it, sent it to the *New Republic*, and they took it! The next clatter out of the box, she asked me if I would go with her up to their office. Of course I said yes. So on a lovely summer day, we started out to walk through Central Park and a little ways further to their building, up a steep, dark flight of steps. Then there we were. Several young men and women welcomed her with open arms and took her into somebody's office. I took a seat in sort of a waiting room. And it wasn't until I got back home in Oregon—no, much longer—that I realized I had been on hallowed ground again, at least to the famous authors who wrote about their connections with THE *New Republic*.

I didn't see Anzia too much after that. Once I took her to a shoe store to have something done to a pair of shoes she had bought there, and while she was busy somewhere in the store, the clerk came over to me and asked, "How did you ever get mixed up with a woman like that?" Then he said, "She's the meanest old woman in New York!" Ripeness might not have been all with her, but I never found her mean. But the clerk fairly trembled when we came in with her shoes, and she said she couldn't catch the exterminator because he always hid. I'm glad she had that triumph, though, with her story about the bird flying in her window, which must have been one of her last.

HERMAN THOUGHT IT WAS wonderful how a writer would set out to write a story about nothing. But better to do what I was doing and lie fallow for a year or two until I had something to say, he said. It's a lot longer than a year or two, I didn't remind him; it's more like ten. It's so long that that's why I got in touch with the witch. A declaration like that would have frozen his blood, though, so I kept still. And he didn't ask what I was working on, because he had met Wittgenstein and knew how to deal with so-called creative people. I had a hunch he was taking into consideration what a writer like me—assuming because of my books that I *was* a writer—might make if somebody else cooked the meals and kept house (him, for instance), and just let them *work*. People like Colette and types like that. In fact, he asked me how productive I thought I might be under circumstances like those. Of course I said I didn't know, thinking as I spoke of the workroom I had had specially built (with the skylight and the suit of lights on the wall) that after a few weeks I couldn't open the door to walk into without wanting to vomit. So it depended, I said. Maybe if I had some really interesting subject matter, like his experiences in World War One—? he said.

Not long after this, his daughter invited us to her house for Sunday dinner, and after we ate we took a stroll along a pretty little canal and looked at her neighbors' big new houses, pretty yards and beautiful trees, and he said the cheapest house you could build there had to cost $65,000, which to me, on my *New York on $5 a Day*, seemed like quite a bit. "Of course, *we* could manage that," he said. You and who else? I didn't say. Then he said he had thought things over and it seemed like the best thing to do was to build a house here by his daughter and get married. That way I would see grandchildren growing up around me, and even if something happened to him (him being twenty years older than me, he didn't say) I need never be alone. That was very nice of him to think like that, I said. But then I thought of how we didn't jibe and how I never could stand Conrad Nagel and said no. It would never have worked, and how disappointed he would have been when he, like what's his name, put Colette to work and nothing came of it.

WHEN I CAME TO NEW YORK, I thought of something on the bus that I might do. A project. I thought of how in the old days in California, the miners had found gold and silver, made millions of dollars, built big mansions, bought racehorses not only to race but to pull their carriages, ate lobster day and night and bought whatever their eye rested on that they wanted. Sometimes what they wanted was a beautiful girl, walking down the street or in a pioneer wagon arriving from Ohio, or just in the open air hanging up a wash, to say nothing of all the other things a beautiful girl might be doing. But whatever, as soon as it could be managed, the miner and the beautiful girl would be wedded and bedded. Then the girl would aspire to show, by her every gesture, word, mannerism and possession, just who she was and what she had attained. This was not easy for everyone, so a so-called "society" woman would open up a school here and there, not just for a daughter who had married beyond herself, but for the mother too, or a widow, or just anyone who could pay. And if they learned their lessons well, they could be "society" women too.

So what I got to wondering on the bus was whether such instruction was available today for young women or old, uneasy in the niche into which good fortune had cast them. I thought that if such lessons were available in New York, I might take some and write an article about it for *Vogue* or maybe *Harper's Bazaar*. Thinking about it on the bus, it didn't seem like something I couldn't do. A little article? And it would be fun to hunt around New York for "society" instruction.

As soon as I could, I consulted my *New York on $5 a Day* guide but found nothing remotely like it. There was a chapter on music and dancing lessons, also cooking, but no mention of decorum, which I guess was what I had in mind. Here is this slob and she wants to be a swan. As I write about it, my project seems like somebody's "idea of nothing to do." But when I got up the nerve to go to *Vogue* headquarters and ask the young lady to whom I had been directed if anybody would be interested in reading an article if I found such a course and took it, middle-aged backwoods lady though I was, and then set forth to do—what, I didn't know, would *Vogue* consider such a report?

"Quaint," the young woman said. "I don't know why not. Do it and send it in." But she said "quaint" again, which such an idea *was*, there in New York in 1964, when everything was in flux—mores, morals, manners, the whole nine yards (myself knowing that *now*, nearly forty years later, but not then)—and that discouraged me a little. How could a 1905 idea like that be quaint?

As I was going out the door, she said: "Oh, by the way, why don't you run in and see Daphne, who does our section on schools? She does the ads for them in the back." Of the magazine, she meant. Private schools, finishing schools for the rich or well-born or powerful, or all three.

Daphne's office, though small and cluttered and without a window, looked just like the rest of what I had seen so far of *Vogue*'s layout—scenes and sets for a movie about America's top fashion magazine, moderne, the colors faux, its smell probably like Elizabeth Taylor. Daphne was a jolly girl like a rowing instructor, quite easy for me to talk to, and when I left her I had two names and addresses.

One was for a Miss Michelle Bourbon, who gave classes about conducting oneself on the Orient Express and in every other high-toned circumstance that a full-spectrum life might offer, at $50 for a term of six lectures. I don't know what her qualifications were, except that she might have been an heir to the French Throne had there still been one. Miss Desfossés was much more expensive, gave private lessons only and was a voice coach and teacher of grace and charm at a prestigious and costly girls' school. I got in touch with both women and signed up for as much instruction as was needed to find out what they were doing and if that would be a help to any living person.

Miss Bourbon, whose name was much longer, but that was the salient part, lived in what looked like quite large quarters in a new apartment house with a doorman. Her apartment was full of artificial flowers so natural you had to touch them to find out they weren't real. She was allergic to actual flowers, and for all I know to sunshine, for it wasn't real either. And her chirp of feathered songsters she turned on and off as needed.

My fellow classmates at Miss Bourbon's were two or three young men in suits and ties, with polished shoes and antebellum haircuts, and three or four young ladies who might have been dressed for presentation by Helen Gurley Brown—deadly serious climbers, you could tell, who had come quite a distance before ever hearing of Miss Bourbon. The two lectures I heard her present—on toasts (how to give and respond to them), how to write letters to grieving nobility and act in banks and on The Week-end—were enough of a sample. I didn't attend the four more lessons I had coming, and perhaps still have for all I know, though Miss Bourbon must be about a hundred years old by now, her flowers shattered and shabby and her songbirds permanently stilled.

MISS DESFOSSÉS AND I became friends of sorts. She turned out to be the real thing—tall, slender, blond hair going white, high-bridged nose, back so straight that even when she was reclining on her couch, like Madame Récamier, her back looked like she had swallowed a sword. Speaking of reclining on a couch, Miss Desfossés was the only person I ever saw do that barefooted while entertaining guests. I don't remember what kind of outfit she had on at the time, but her feet, perfectly pedicured and with every toe in place and almost rouged, looked so dainty and rosy.

Miss Bourbon couldn't have cared less what you were doing, but Miss Desfossés burrowed right in. Who were you? Where did you come from? What were you up to? Soon she knew all about my slithering little moves, she knew about my books and that two were Literary Guild selections, which, much to my surprise, seemed to invoke her to give a small dinner for me with some of her friends as guests. I say much to my surprise because in the forties and even quite a while later, there were only two book clubs in America, the Book-of-the-Month Club and the Literary Guild, and in Portland amongst our bookish cohorts, the one that gave you the brownie points was the former. The Literary Guild was a great deal better than a poke in the eye with a sharp stick, of course, but not something that because of, you could throw your weight around.

So I was surprised at Miss Desfossés's wanting to have this dinner for me like I was Erica Jong or someone. And when the five or six shimmering, sophisticated New Yorkers all appeared, my throat was so dry I could hardly swallow. I don't know what we had to eat, but Miss Desfossés had apparently cooked it beforehand in her little kitchen, and with one of the women helping her, she served it like a picnic, with paper napkins, while classical music played softly in the background. Whether she started out with bare feet is a mystery to me, but when we sipped our coffee, or maybe a bit later when everything had settled down to bright-sounding conversation on the other people's part and Miss Desfossés had gone into this lissome recline on the couch, I noticed these somewhat luminous bare feet and thought that this was society indeed.

And in a way it really was: one of my fellow guests sat by me and fed me something with his fingers—I can't think what, or how I ever swallowed it, I was so tense and nervous all of a sudden. A handsome young man in his late twenties, I should say, with a beautiful wife, he was the actor Paul Roebling. Being an actor in famous plays and movies—a real one, talking the talk, with an actress wife—would have been enough to dine out on for a month, as Oscar Wilde would say. But Mr. Roebling was also the great-grandson of the man who built the Brooklyn Bridge, and I don't know how you could have much more of a claim to fame than that alone. *The Bridge!*

Later, Miss Desfossés told me he had come to her for voice lessons. She didn't know who he was, just this sweet young man. But later they became true friends, and once when he picked her up in his car (any car his little heart desired, of course) at the school where she worked and they started out, he said would she mind if he stopped at his place to pick up something? She said no, of course not, and where was his place? Shall I tell you? *The Plaza.* He and his wife lived there! So that was when Miss Desfossés found out about his being the world-renowned bridge builder's great-grandson. I would probably have heard more about him and his mother, a much-publicized world banker, and what she did to him psychically and all kinds of information, if Miss Desfossés, after many years in New York, had not been stricken with a detached retina and a mysterious lump on the side of her head or some such thing, and had to pull up stakes and return to Canada, where, being a descendant of Lord Lovat, who was beheaded in 1747, she was not unknown. That ended my grand scheme to become a woman of the world and write for *Vogue.*

My nephew Michael, he and his wife being aspiring thespians, enjoyed hearing about Paul Roebling, a sweet person just like you and me. Michael knew somebody who had been in Rome when Paul was there and who had even appeared in a movie Paul was in before this other actor's part was cut out. Michael's wife, Judy—his girlfriend and fellow actor at Portland State University a few years before this—already belonged to Equity, and they were now about to go and do summer stock in some well-known summer spot. Almost as if they had read all the books, they lived a life like two actors in a play about moving from the Far West to New York City to get on the stage. A tiny apartment in MacDougal Street seemed to be waiting for them, where they could just step across the street to a restaurant and here would be this famous person or that one just having dinner or a drink. And the famous model Marion Morehouse, married to the famous poet E. E. Cummings, who wrote about her that "nobody, not even the rain, has such small hands."

Immortal words! and here she was like a human woman going past to the grocery store!

Michael and Judy didn't have a bathtub, but a stationary tub with a wooden lid on it in the kitchen that they could hop into and take a bath. Some of Judy's fellow actors even came sometimes and took a bath—dancers, mostly, that somehow found the deep old tub hard to get out of and would holler for help from Michael, who would come and shut his eyes and lift them out. He and Judy got ahead in the theater quite a bit quicker than the average newcomers, but somehow they didn't stay the course; they left to become drama professors and directors, Michael at Fordham University at Lincoln Center and Judy at Reed College in her old hometown of Portland. But at first it seemed like fate had set everything up, almost like a movie script, for them to advance in a certain way and become—who? They like who they are now—Michael very successful, with a beautiful blond second wife—so don't even ask. Still, I blink and swallow a lump down my throat for the raggle-taggle gypsy O! they were, and the actors and Cocqcigrues they seemed by way of becoming in those old pied days of yore.

You don't have to pay money and take lessons to learn new stuff. But you have to be out amongst it, and I was, when I learned that the act of applauding and showing one's appreciation for a performance, say, is as different from one époque to another as night from day.

A new acquaintance from San Francisco, sent to look me up by another friend who lived there—where if you aren't with it during life's every moment, you might as well be dead—came one evening and took me to a Sonny Rollins concert. Sonny just starts in and plays his saxophone along uncharted paths, like the great god Pan in a dark forest, till he gets tired and quits. And while the audience, many of them dressed and looking like some of Miss Bourbon's anxious pupils, sat as if stunned, I clapped and made remarks to Sanders—that was my escort's name—and smiled and exclaimed, so that Sonny wouldn't be discouraged and have his feelings hurt and give up his career. When we walked home, Sanders told me gently that at concerts like Sonny Rollins's, people didn't clap and carry on anymore like they used to. So I was glad to know that.

I learned a lot about books and records and art from Sanders, and if he hadn't died of a broken heart (so I heard) many years ago, I would say thank you and tell him that being friends with him was one of the best parts about my dreamtime in New York. We went to museums—Huntington Hartford's with the twenty-foot-high painting by Salvador Dali of Jesus' cross that looks like it's going to come crashing down on you— and I don't know where all, and he thought I was just a genius the way I had discovered all these wonderful places to eat so reasonably, and the free entertainment and so on. Oh, Sanders, if it were now I would share *New York on $5 a Day* and every-thing with you.

The word "homosexual" seems like an old word, doesn't it? But I was reading the other day that Freud was thirteen years old before it was even invented. In those days, people didn't talk about whatever came to mind the way they do now, and Sanders and I never mentioned his not liking girls, or anything along that line of country at all.

He was very excited about the World's Fair being almost ready to open and said if the restaurant in the Americana, where he worked as a waiter, didn't open a branch at the Fair, he was going to quit and try to get on with somebody else out there. Every day the paper had something about the World's Fair, and so, no doubt, did television. It was going to amaze the entire population of the earth. Kings, queens, presidents and I don't know who all were coming, including the most celebrated scientists, because science was what the Fair was all about. New York went along as usual, waiting. The gallants still tried to strike up an acquaintance with girls, and even women getting up in years like me. They would approach you smilingly, and as they went past would say something like "I will do anything you want."

Once a nicely dressed man approached me in Central Station and, tipping his hat, said, "May I ask you something?" I nodded cordially, thinking he wanted directions (which I'm sure I wouldn't have been able to give). "How do you keep the men away from you?" he said. When you turned away or left quickly, they never tried to follow you. Making remarks was just what they did. Gentlemen you dealt with would try a little boldness, too, and you soon learned that making a painter or carpenter a cup of coffee and perching for a chat might not be the best policy. Once the brother and business partner of the carpenter who built my twelve-foot-high bookcase came looking for him at close to suppertime and found him flat on his back on the floor under my coffee table (which had been hurt in transit and which he was slowly fixing) and sent him home forthwith, as the saying goes. The brother left, too, but came back to tell me that his brother was a *married man*, that they and all their relatives lived in the same building in the apartments they had taken over one by one as they came from the old country. They never had to close their doors and everything was going along fine, and they didn't want a lot of—the word he was trying to say I presume was shenanigans, but I didn't help him with it. After a while the first brother came back for the second brother. There was quite a bit of talk in Italian (Calabrian), and then they went peacefully home. I could imagine the sounds that greeted them with all the open doors, yelling kinfolk, cats, babies, voice pupils, radios, phonographs and televisions.

THE PRESIDENTIAL CAMPAIGN was in full swing. Herman— who, as I mentioned earlier, should in the natural order of things have been a Republican—was an analytic Democrat and listened to every political speech or discussion he could find on TV, and had we been closer, he would have been disappointed that I hardly seemed to know who was running. Now I care quite a bit about politics, but then there seemed to be too much else going on to pay attention. My mother's father was a Democrat, but amidst vox populi, his voice didn't carry far. The reason for this was that during a time of high indignation against the Mormons for polygamy, Grandpa was arrested for having two wives; he was tried and sentenced to six months in prison. Prison, not jail, where they had to wear stripes (going around, not up and down, so that in case they escaped they could be easily spotted) and break stones and have a hard time in general. Not least was the embarrassment for Grandpa, a quite prosperous merchant tailor. But several Mormons high up in the church were serving time at the same time Grandpa was, and that made him proud, particularly when they asked him to join them in prayer and conversation. The day they were let go, the warden gave a speech and said if all his prisoners were as gentlemanly as they were, instead of like the usual riffraff and hooligans, he wouldn't even know he was working. Then they lined up shoulder to shoulder, about a dozen of them altogether, and a photographer took their picture. Of course Grandpa put in an order—for two pictures, one for each wife. The first wife just stuck up her nose, but Grandma had her picture framed and hung up in her front parlor. And once—this was the part of the mythology that we all liked—a recent convert to the church from England came to visit Grandma, and when she saw the horizontal stripes in the picture, she clasped her hands, for it reminded her of home: "Oh! A cricket team!" she said happily.

But the funny part to us descendants, though not to Grandpa, was what happened then. Utah soon became a state, and not only a state but one giving women the vote. So Grandpa, who having been in prison was a felon and could never vote the Democratic or any other kind of ticket again, might have felt terrible had he not had the ace in the hole of having two wives to vote in his place. But the best-laid plans—! Each wife went to her precinct (naturally located far apart) and *voted Republican*, this being the dearest wish of the hearts of the highest mucky-mucks of the church. And Republican they stayed, both these wives and most of the other female voters, all their lives.

When I told this to Herman one time, he smiled politely and said polygamy put such a burden on men that he couldn't understand how anyone would go into it. And basically so silly, when it was so simple for men and women to be romantically friendly.

SPEAKING OF WHICH, I almost told him about a guest I expected to entertain when the time came by taking him to the World's Fair. But I didn't, because Herman and Ernesto—Egon's cousin, who had written me he was coming to New York about when the Fair was to open—were both smarties, and I wasn't necessarily going to introduce them. Ernesto's wife had died in 1956, and Ernesto, on a world tour soon after, had come to visit Egon and me in Portland. Not for long, for which I was happy, for it was about then that I was trying desperately to make my attic workroom work. It wouldn't, and I was a poor hostess. But Egon enjoyed seeing his old cousin for the brief while he was there, took him around and showed him the sights, and after he was gone told me all the things they had talked about. Mostly girls ("girls," I say—Ernesto was then about sixty-three or four, but he was a real Lothario, which Egon hadn't seemed to know until now that Ernesto was a widower). Coming from a rich and worldly branch of the family, he had had a mistress when he was fifteen and one ever since, from a lot of different categories—the ballet, artists' models and such as that (if he didn't make it all up). And when his father and uncles set up business in Buenos Aires and put him in charge of some of it, he became acquainted with a lot of beautiful brunettes, which he hadn't particularly cultivated before, and eventually married one, from Vienna like him. They were very happy, had no children and lived in a fashionable apartment with rooms so large that their living room could contain not one but two grand pianos of the largest size.

Ernesto's wife, Adele, was the musician in the family, just for the family's amusement, and neither she nor Ernesto ever missed anything of musical significance if they could help it. Many such events came along, with world-famous musicians, as Buenos Aires audiences were well known for their zeal and devotion and not caring how much the tickets cost. Eventually Ernesto and Adele, always in the front row, got acquainted with certain of these itinerant performers and offered some of their rooms as a place to come and practice, especially when they needed two great big pianos standing side by side. How much this furthered Ernesto's romantic aspirations I don't know, but divas and dancers and virtuosos of all kinds took advantage of the arrangement, and both of their hosts felt honored by the custom, especially when their rooms were pictured in local newspapers and magazines. It lasted a long time, perhaps even up until the time Adele got sick with some kind of wasting and long-lasting disease and eventually died. If what Ernesto told Egon was true, polygamy—whether with two wives or with fifty-six, like Brigham Young—would have restricted him a lot. In his letter about coming to New York, he said "we" several times, so he had either remarried or was being accompanied by a *petite amie*, though he was seventy or more by now. A spry seventy, judging by his liveliness a few years before, but I dreaded taking him to the Fair less than I would have if I hadn't been in such fine fettle from walking around New York with Sanders.

A FEW DAYS BEFORE I was thinking this, Sanders and I had gone to Carnegie Hall for a free talk about the famous Duncan family of San Francisco, of which Isadora was a member. With the Jackson family, or Utah's Donny and Marie conglomeration, it isn't hard to see why they were famous. They sang, danced, acted and I don't know what all. But in the case of the six or seven stair-step Duncans wandering Europe like gypsy tinkers, all they seemed to do, boys and girls alike, was let their hair grow, go barefoot, strike what were thought to be Grecian poses, eat natural foods if they could get them, not wear anything binding, and be, one and all, of such red-gold Celtic beauty that when they appeared, it seemed like a flock of angels had landed. Isadora, the youngest, was the most beautiful, and as the little band wandered here and there, she got the most attention, lecturing about natural living and trying to teach collections of lovely maidens how to dance in their bare feet and be brave and stand up for themselves and not be pushed around like their Irish or Scottish father had pushed the Duncans around.

Isadora refused to understand when she was being courted and was beyond the age of consent, whatever that might have been, when in Paris she finally gave heed to the importuning of the heir to the Singer Sewing Machine empire. Whether she would rather have been married to him than stay single while they lived their lives of luxury and she had two beautiful children, a boy and a girl, she does not say in her book about herself. But when the Singer heir left her after the children drowned in the Seine—they were sitting in the family limousine waiting for Isadora to come back from shopping when the brakes the chauffeur hadn't locked tight enough gave way and they rolled helplessly to their deaths—Isadora thought it was so cruel that she doubted for a while if there was a God. But not for long; godlessness does not go with the Celtic nature. Her lover never came back, and after basking in the Singer fortune, it was hard to live, in a manner of speaking, off the land. But she lectured and gathered her maidens for instruction and stayed as beautiful as the dawn, even if somewhat fat. And when she was fifty, one summer evening an admirer came by in an open car, and when she got in the back seat and the chauffeur started them off, the long scarf tied around her neck was blown by a gust of wind into the back wheel well, where it became entangled and gave such a jerk that it strangled her and broke her neck.

I would have thought Carnegie Hall would be as full for a lecture about the Duncan family and Isadora—with one of the boys, Raymond, there in person to shake hands and say hello—as for a concert by what's his name, the violinist so fast and furious that it was rumored he had sold his soul to the devil. But no. When Sanders and I got there, there were only seven or eight people sitting around in the famous seats that had held Diamond Jim Brady and other celebrities too numerous to mention. After quite a long wait, several people came out on the stage with a long, gaunt old man in what looked like not a wheelchair, but more like a beach chair such as they push summer visitors in; it was Raymond Duncan, in his eighties or nineties. He had on sort of a toga that fell open here and there, showing bare bones, wrinkles, and sad loose spots. The free lecture didn't last long, and when it was over the speaker said if anyone wanted, they could come up on the stage and speak to Raymond.

For the first time in my life, as I never like to put myself forward, I stood up and then actually went up on that hallowed, shabby, dusty, neglected-looking stage—if my memory weren't shot, I could tell you all the famous feet, including Jenny Lind's, that had trod it—and there I was, and there was Raymond Duncan, and will wonders never cease. Close up, he looked like the old man of the mountain, without a beard but with grey and white bristles on his chin and cheeks. Also, he looked as if he had been out in the loamy fields; his bare feet, in true Grecian sandals, looked really dirty, and his toes—like fingers, with more joints than a lot of toes—had dirt in, under, and around the long nails. I don't know who had given the talk or who the entourage was up there. All I could think of was everything at once—me standing on the stage at Carnegie Hall, then down on my knees beside the summer chair, and Raymond and I holding hands after we shook hands and didn't let go, and Isadora and Mr. Singer of the sewing machine my mother had, and the two babies in the car rolling down into the Seine, and the times and Isadora's billowing scarf in the dusk and how everything was. Raymond said I could go with them wherever they were going, but Sanders came and helped me up, and then we were walking outside and the New York sun was setting and the lights coming on . . . Oh, my God, don't you always think you know? What's it all about, Alfie?

As I say, Sanders and I walked a lot and saw different things and talked. I seemed to have made a momentous discovery at just that time because of suddenly seeing, as if for the first time, what happened in my neighborhood. And that is, nothing. People just went about their business. The lady in the cleaning shop was always there. The owner (or whoever he was) of the apartment house where, I'd heard, two boys hung themselves together over their open closet door was always at his right front downstairs window, looking out. Miss Berger and Mr. Raven, my landlord, who had fought and been so brave in the Spanish war against Franco and his cardinals and had sacrificed his eyesight, took their seats every morning at nine o'clock in their tiny business office with life-size, beautiful blue-eyed Mr. Raven, painted by Moses Soyer, standing behind them. And there they sat quietly all day, while across the hall his wife tended to the babies. And so it went—the man in the fish store, the lady who ran the bodega, the coffee-shop man. Even the people who didn't work worked. What I mean to say is, how many ordinary people, going about their life's business, went to the library? How many went and bought tickets for *Tiny Alice* or *Othello* or whatever was going on in Madison Square Garden? Millions, maybe, but the same amount, or more, *didn't* go. They stayed home, took a walk around the block, had got up early so went to bed betimes. They got up, tended to business. It wasn't just going and doing and killing themselves every minute, but just living.

"So what?" Sanders said when I tried to tell him. "Well, nothing, only— Take me. I came to New York, going to the library, the famous library, where all the writers— Shows. It's hard work to get dressed up and go places evenings. The opera. I got here in January and now the summer is almost over and I've only been twice. I haven't even got myself together to go uptown to see a movie. Or fashion shows. Things cost a lot, but not only in money—in time, too. So anyway, what I've dis- covered is that people don't do half as many extracurricular activities as television and papers and magazines make us think they do. It's expensive, but more than that—if you are honest, it wears a person out, and what do you have to show for it? Most people just do their daily rounds and that's it."

"I suppose next I'll hear you're not going to the World's Fair, when it's practically in our lap," Sanders said.

"Oh, I'm going. But my other discovery—New York isn't big at all, it's little."

"Tell Lindsay that," Sanders said.

"It's just this one little village, even Times Square, even Beekman Place, repeated over and over hundreds and thousands of times. Little hamlets. All nestled up against each other, people stay in them the way they do in villages. You see, if you live in one, they're there. But the *effect* is of one great big terrifying *city*, an immense, full-spectrum, rattling, teeming place. But it isn't. It's just—villages. But we don't know. We say *New York* and shake in our shoes."

(A few months after I got back home in Portland, I read a piece in *Harper's* magazine or somewhere that said practically the same thing, only sparklingly and with say-so like a high intelligence.)

"I suppose next I'll hear you're going home," Sanders said.

"Why would I do that?" Indeed, I hadn't thought of it. Not really. But then one day I thought how the beautiful rain would soon be coming down and the mists blow in from the sea and I wouldn't be there. And it seemed like I had made a wrong turn somewhere and might have to look sharp not to be lost.

NEW YORK ON $5 A DAY had nothing much to offer as regards the Fair, now within just days of opening. Ernesto wrote that "we" were looking forward to New York but that their plans kept changing or being added to. However, he would call me when they arrived, and he was looking forward to our day at the Fair.

Sanders, as he had said he was going to do, quit his job at the most posh of the restaurants in the Americana and hung up the tailcoat the waiters there had to wear, and he was going out to the Fair to see a restaurant captain about a job that was practically promised him in an elegant spin-off of the Four Seasons. It seemed quite late in the day to me, but the day before the Fair was to open, the call he had waited for came, and

he invited me to go with him out to Flushing Meadows. He
didn't actually have the job, but things thus far had gone
forward enough to elate him, and he showed up at my
apartment with his brown hair dyed coal black with Miss
Clairol—easiest thing in the world, he said, took five minutes.
He wore a beautiful Brooks Brothers rented suit (apparently
you can rent other kinds of clothes besides tuxedos if you know
where) and so hopeful a mien that he almost looked like he had
makeup on.

When we got there, it might as well have been Carthage, or
the empire's own great city, going up to the sound of
hammering, banging, and pulsing machinery, with a motley
crew of workmen and well-dressed proprietary individuals of
every description—like a captured nation transported to toil
forever, running around, climbing on what appeared to be
pulleys and high wires, then swinging down, water running,
lights flashing . . . The papers said it was all ready for tomorrow, every last detail, but amidst the hubbub of the way we
wended, over fresh green grass and with the smell of flowers
and manure, it didn't seem so.

Sanders had got directions, so he knew right where he was
going to see this Four Seasons captain and where to leave me
till he came back. This latter was an immensely high-ceilinged
hall of some kind, like a theater with rows of seats and a big
stage, with its curtain up if it had one, which I presume it did.
On the stage was a large, handsome armchair with a large, life-
like, handsomely suited, shirted and bowtied Abraham Lincoln
sitting in it among several members of the captured nation, who
were moving about tossing off remarks to one another. I had
read several reports in the paper about this Lincoln robot that
could not only sit and cross its legs, walk, talk, hold forth its
hand, and recite its most famous declaration, but also look right
at you and smile with a twinkle in its eye, as if it knew you
voted for him. So I was very interested and took a good look.
But Lincoln wasn't doing anything, so I watched the tired-
looking men on the stage and a few people who tiptoed in and
out as though in the 1864 White House, speaking in hushed

tones, and I wondered how long it was going to take Sanders to make his contact.

Time went by, and pretty soon I saw that the captured nation was moving about more purposefully than before and was setting something up, or trying to set something up, with Lincoln. He was supposed to be very heavy with all the electronic wonders inside him, and at six feet four inches tall might not have been the stablest robot ever to wear shoe leather. But the workmen hovering around pressed buttons and sashayed about, there was a whirring and a strangled word or two, and the next thing I knew, here was Lincoln in his fine black broadcloth getting tremblingly to his feet as though he hadn't moved for a long time, and, not entirely unlike Frankenstein's monster, was taking a step, gradually turning, taking another step and another until "No! No!" one of the workmen cried and ran over and grabbed him as the others began to converge. Well, it was as if grabbing ahold of him like that scared Lincoln, and he pushed the man away and then it was like a cartoon where all the characters mix together in what looks like a whirling ball, and arms and legs fly out. Then you could see they had Lincoln on the floor, he never should have been startled like that in the first place and he was fighting like a tiger. His contenders were hollering, sweating and panting. And then he just gave up and lay still, and everybody took stock. And then they helped him up and helped him gently and politely to his chair, where he sat awhile to get himself in order. And then, not so shakily this time, he gradually sat up very straight, then stood up, and this time walked the right way in the right direction to a sort of table, beside which he planted his feet, held out his hand, opened his lips and said, "Four score and seven years ago," then went right on to give the speech, then turned and, slow as the seven-year itch, retraced his steps. But that was all right, people were smiling and clapping. And he sat down. I had gone up close by then, and as he and I exchanged glances, it was like we were in Ford's theater and he hadn't been shot, he was alive—living and would live forever, and my heart just almost burst.

Sanders came after me a little while later. He hadn't got the job, but his contact said they would put him on their emergency list. So that was a disappointment, and all the way home he seemed downcast and didn't seem to want to talk about Lincoln breaking loose or anything.

I HEARD WHO "WE" WAS the next day when Ernesto phoned. He and Antoinette had arrived and were staying that night at the Plaza but were going to be picked up tomorrow by the chauffeur of one of his partners, to be taken to the man's country place. We made up a day to go to the Fair, but Ernesto didn't think Antoinette was going to be able to make it, as she had quite a schedule. But he and I could go. I said, did she have a lot of friends in New York? and he said it wasn't that exactly. Well, I said, would he and she like to come to dinner one night? I had been practicing and wasn't quite as terrible a cook as when he visited us in Oregon. Unfortunately, that wouldn't be possible, he said, and maybe he had better count on just the one day at the Fair, because when they took care of all they had to do, they were going to push right off for Europe, Paris and then Barcelona. "Am I not going to meet Antoinette?" I said. "Well, she made all these appointments," he said lamely. A house didn't have to fall on me, so I said well, perhaps some other time—when you come back.

But I was curious, and when the day came for him and me to go to the Fair, he told me as we walked around that thank goodness, in another three or four days she would be a free woman, and after a shopping trip or two— Though as she said, who would want to shop in New York when they were on their way to Paris and Barcelona? "Free woman?" I said. "Ernesto, you have to tell me what's going on or I'll die." And over lunch in the gorgeous restaurant where Sanders didn't get a job, he did.

Antoinette was only in her forties, so beautiful that famous producers, Ernesto didn't know how many, had tried to put her in their movies, but as she always said, she was happy as she was. As well she might have been, with an adoring husband of many years who was one of Ernesto's partners, a besotted lover, maids, furs, diamonds, anything she wanted at her command. But beauty doesn't come with a lifetime guaranty, and finally her mirror stopped saying, "You— You— " Then she had to find out what all science had been up to in the beauty line. When they arrived, she had checked into one of New York's most costly and exclusive hospitals to have several world-famous surgeons, in a series of meticulous operations, lift, pull, stretch, cut, stitch, fix and sew and return her to her understanding (if somewhat dull-witted) husband and her lover, whose favorite thing in life was beautiful women and who thought Antoinette was the most beautiful woman of all. Poor little pet, vomiting because of the anesthetic over and over, black and blue, swollen, could hardly take in nourishment—but *so brave*. It really made you bow down to them, their courage, never a word of complaint. Well, he would make it up to her, Ernesto said.

HE AND I WENT AROUND on the tramway in an open sight-seeing car and saw everything. Ernesto was always on the lookout for new things to take over and make money on, so even though he was now so old he had to sit down and rest and would fan himself every now and then with his hand—and at one of the fountains he wet his handkerchief and touched it to his temples—he examined everything from top to bottom. When he seemed like he was gasping for air, I got somewhat afraid that he might keep on till he collapsed.

Finally, I mentioned a feature at this very fair that I had read about which appealed to me but which I hadn't intended to mention, because it seemed so chicken-livered. And what that was, was a concession called— I don't remember the name, but what it consisted of, you bought a key for quite an exorbitant price, unlocked a muslin door, went in and had a beautiful little shady, air-cooled bedroom with a tiny bathroom with a shower, and a narrow cot with smooth, comfortable, white paper sheets and two lovely down pillows, so you could take your clothes off and nap, and then freshen up and be as good as new again.

You couldn't go in these bowers except by yourself, and when the chime sounded at a quarter to your hour, you had to get up and be gone, unless you wanted to pay for another hour. But the little rooms were so cool that usually one hour was enough. It gave you such a fresh start that to me, that concession was the best one on the fairgrounds. You could rest, you know, and while I was dozing off in my cool paper sheets I thought of a poem, I couldn't think whose, with "rest" in it that ended "And that will be the best." It does sound wimpy, doesn't it? But I persuaded Ernesto to try a little surcease from all the wonders, and when we met outside the concession, he said it had been refreshing. What won't they think of next?

ERNESTO WAS SO PLEASED to have seen everything and recuperated that he invited me to a little evening at the home of a relative of his partner (the one with the country house), in the 600 block on Fifth Avenue. Several people were there when we arrived, quietly sitting around talking politics. After I had been there awhile, I moved to sit close to an elderly woman who was sitting in a high-backed chair looking out of a long window that went clear to the floor. She turned out to be the host's mother. "You're not the beauty," she greeted me.

"No," I said.

"How is she?"

"I don't know. I've never met her."

"Well, all I know," she said, "I never heard of somebody having to have round-the-clock hospital nursing for a week or two for just a facelift. That Ernesto!" she said.

"He was a cousin of my husband's," I said. After we had covered that quite extensively, due to her questions, she said that her family and Ernesto's had been neighbors in Vienna, so she knew Ernesto quite well. In fact, when her brother and Ernesto were both young men, they had gone into partnership. Buying up nacre.

"Nacre?" I said.

"Mother of pearl," she said. "They traveled around the Bosporus buying up all they could find for a button factory

Ernesto later owned. They went everywhere. And you could never imagine what happened when they got to Constantinople. That was 1921 or something like that. The Sultan had been dethroned and Ataturk was about to take over the country. From what Felix said—he's the brother I'm talking about, Ernesto's age, lives in London, he hates it here. But anyway, from what Felix said, Constantinople was like a smashed beehive, all the people that owned and ran everything had left, everybody else too, and here these two boys were, wandering around.

"So they just kept going, and the next thing they knew here they were at the Sultan's palace, and what did they find but the place was deserted, the doors open, unlocked, nobody standing guard, all the rooms empty. So they went in and pretty soon they were in the harem, where the harem ladies lived. The boys could tell that by the mess they left, the scents and everything. But the birds themselves had flown. All except two, whom they discovered in a sort of sunroom, one sitting on a divan and the other at a window watching out for someone to come and get her. The news had got out, and most of the ladies had been picked up by their relatives or gone somewhere. These two women, like all the others, had been picked for their beauty and had come from Bessarabia and ten other places, even England and Sweden. So the two ladies that Felix and Ernesto had stumbled upon in the palace were so much more beautiful than anybody they had ever seen before that they were almost blinded. But Felix was a terrible exaggerator and Ernesto wasn't far behind, so none of us paid much attention when they told us of this adventure. Her brother or someone came for the girl at the window and the boys looked after the one on the divan, who was the most beautiful of the two, and found shelter for her and fed her like a turtledove. Both of them fell in love with her—"

"And Ernesto got her," I guessed.

"No, he didn't," the old woman said. "Felix was much better-looking, if you'll pardon my saying so."

"I don't mind a bit," I said. "What happened?"

"Truth can be stranger than fiction."

"I've heard that," I said.

"We didn't meet her, but Felix set her up somewhere, I think. But I had no more than heard of her when the next news we had was that our uncle or someone had sent Felix to Russia, and the harem girl—who didn't turn out to be that young, although so very handsome—was with child."

"With child?" I said.

"By now five or six months along," she said. "And Felix had only known her since the government collapsed in Constantinople, about a month. So the baby couldn't be his." She paused. "Whose could it be?"

"The Sultan's?" I ventured.

"Maybe a eunuch's, my uncle said," she replied. "Those eunuchs weren't always perfect."

"She wouldn't know how to work," I said. "At a job. If she had to fend for herself."

"Work?" she said. "She'd have fainted if you said the word. But it all turned out all right."

"Oh?" I said. "How was that?"

Pausing to think, she shifted in her chair. "You can say what you want about Ernesto, but he behaved better than Felix. One word from my uncle and off he went to Russia. But Ernesto—"

"She became his mistress."

"No, that's too easy," the old lady said. "He told me that the fact she was the last one left should have told them something, and he wondered why they had packed up her little property and brought her to Vienna. Exuberance, I guess. They knew they had done well with the nacre purchases, which indeed they had—that was the start of some immediate success for both of them, though they were never chums again the way they once had been."

"Ernesto married her."

She laughed. "Oh, yes. And our Empress ate an entire sixteen-course dinner! No, but he took care of her, and when the baby was born, he sent her home to Croatia or wherever she came from and gave the baby to their family cook or housekeeper, or whatever she was, to raise. But the child turned out so lovely that she couldn't have been the Sultan's. I met him at a Christmas ball in the palace one time, and his face would have stopped a clock. Once, when she was about six, Ernesto, on the spur of the moment, brought her a doll or something, and after that he really watched over her, had her educated. It was like that movie with Leslie Caron—she was like a daughter to him. Adele was fit to be tied, as your saying goes, to see them hugging and kissing, so happy to see each other after Antoinette, as Ernesto had named her, had been away in Switzerland to school—and then he found her a husband no one need be ashamed of, and Antoinette and Ernesto became just like King Lear with whichever daughter was his favorite."

"Antoinette," I said. Then, "Do you mean to tell me that this Antoinette you're telling me about is the one with the facelift in the hospital? Whose mother was the last one left in the Sultan's harem?"

None other, the old woman didn't say, but she smiled and the words hung in the air.

"Where are they with the coffee?" she said then, fretfully. "I don't like to drink it too late."

I WENT TO THE WORLD'S FAIR several more times, though not again to the cooling bower with the soft white sheets.

And at election time, when I was making an excuse to a new acquaintance for not registering in time to vote, a filling came out of my tooth and I thought of my dentist in Portland. Three generations doing the same thing in as superior a manner as possible. All that accumulated knowledge, the inherited skills.

And then I was on a bus—one of the fifty ways the song said I could leave my lover, Manhattan—and heading homeward. *New York on $5 a Day* doesn't mention dentists, or a doctor, caskets or markers. And sometimes all these are needed at once. But *carpe diem*, as the old woman said when she peed in the sea. Without witches or anyone, I might even have a workroom again that *this time* would in all its parts, you know, work.

But I didn't think of that, riding and dozing along. Good grief, people were always making things, wonders, marvels and multi-purpose absurdities till they're piled up to the sky! enough for a World's Fair somewhere on feverish Earth, binary coded and artificially intelligenced, every five minutes. It really should stop for a while.

And on the bus, growing dark with Nebraska dusk, my eyelids felt weighted and I sagged into the white goods of the Sikh (that was what he said he was) beside me, then inclined again against the window and thought how Alice was always trying to find the key and get into the beautiful garden, while I . . . got in without even trying. Into the bower, that is, the starched cot, cool pillows and sideshow shadows, the not-a-sound-to-be-heard . . . The resonant and new at its neatest, cleverness banished, mechanics and its ilk shut out, smart-alecky-ness as well, not even music, a fountain's or any other kind. No— going— gone—

"And that will be the best."

# *Appendix: Ardyth's Letters from New York*

Ardyth was a prolific correspondent, but the only letters she wrote from New York that have survived were to her literary friend in Portland, Frederic Oral "Freddy" Jacobson. Freddy's mother gave these cards and letters back to Ardyth after he died in 1990. They were all addressed to Mr. Frederic Jacobson, 1963 N.W. Irving, Portland, Oregon. The letters are in a private family collection.

Ardyth did not always date her letters, and the postmarks on these envelopes and postcards were rarely fully legible, so some of the following dates are approximations.

*Ardyth's first address in New York was 35 East 38th St., Apt. 6-D.*

POSTCARD; 1963, POSSIBLY APRIL

The other day a bi-colored python rock snake pressed right up against me (snakeskin raincoat) and I thought of you, how you'd have got right off that 5th Ave. bus & no fooling. [. . .] An apt. dropped right into my lap the 2nd day I was here, *much* better than where I was going, & O I needed to be IN somewhere, so I took it, at 35 East 38th. This is just the glory that was Greece that's all & if you don't come here you're dippy.

Love, A.

POSTCARD; 1963

Forgot to say—agent very nice. St. Martin's Press nibbling on that book—but seems so long ago & far away, hardly know what they're talking about. By the way, about work here—find I can pop up afterwards without needing decompression & into the world, people, etc. Lovely feeling.

Love, A.

[P.S.] Current favorite book: Of Time, Work & Leisure. We're real groovy with our frowsting, did you know?

LETTER; 1963, PROBABLY EARLY MAY

Thursday

Dear Freddy,

When I sent you that card I was going to write a letter that very evening, in answer to yours. [. . .] But this & that came up—I was going to go & see Sundays with Cybèle. A funny thing—the evening of the day I got your letter Michael called & said Aunt Ardyth, yesterday Judy and I went to the most *wonderful* movie, it's just our kind of—and I guessed—and it was—so we're all on the same wave length. But I haven't seen it yet. Saw Emlyn Williams in A Man for All Seasons, & Dorothy Thompson & Sinclair Lewis's *own child*, playing Henry the VIIIth not 20 feet off. Well, I nearly go out of my mind about half the time. "Nothing like [this] ever was . . ."

So I am flying home—did you get that?—paleolithic me *flying home*—feeling about as proud (if I make it) as a Zuni kid when he gets through that puberty rite that initiates him into the tribe—on March 30th. Got my ticket already—leaving here at 6:30 p.m., arriving 10:30. You're the only one who knows— will tell Mother when I call her on Mother's Day—that I'm coming. I *won't* tell her, and how am I going to break the news, that it's only to sell the house, car, books & everything except a few keepsakes and come back to the one place where—in all my life—I haven't felt like an exile, a displaced person. "Excuse my earnestness"—

You'd feel the same. And now I realize Portland was like a cold, forbidding stepmother—gave me a roof over my head, enough to eat—even vitamins—but no love; and you could never please her.

I haven't told Marion either. My pen here sort of falters when I think of it . . . So don't say anything.

Gee, I went right in to Tiffany's and bought some stationery. I should have used it, to write you on—but I'll tell you what I'll do—write the name of the poet I'm going to hear lecture tonight on a sheet of the paper & use one of the envelopes. And guess who I'm going to hear Sunday? Robert Penn Warren. And when I go to his exhibition I may get to glimpse Man Ray.

Imagine—you read the book reviews on Sunday, walk into Brentano's Monday & there they are. They don't have to send for them. You don't have to wait two weeks.

And guess what I've got? A library card.

All my plans, remember? Well, what a sea change. Have worked, gone to shows, but mostly just stood—or walked—and stared. Every morning when I wake up I'm an Aztec & the Empire State Bldg. is Pococatapetl. One thing I feel bad about— was going to send presents to everybody; even knew what I was going to say with 'em: "Presents" (Dickens) "presents, as I always say, endear absents." But you get impecunious here quick, what with doormen in striped vests that sound like Eric Blore & this & that cropping up (even at home where the Gossers' water heater had to be replaced) & the first thing you know you're figuring all the time. But the bus fares are so cheap—only 15¢—imagine—& the greatest actors in the world will give you a whole afternoon of their time for about $6.

Oh, the sins of *o*mission & *com*mission: didn't call anybody I was supposed to, met other people instead—But when I come back—

Freddy, dear, thank you for writing so sweetly. Did you always make E's like that, even in the old days when you wrote poetry? Well, I have some examples & when I am going through the gleanings of a lifetime, many things for the last time, I shall come across yours—while sifting & sorting—and shall see.

Got to run—take care—

Love, Ardyth

[Handwritten in the middle of a separate sheet, on stationery that matches the envelope:] Robert Graves

POSTCARD; MAY 1963

Wasn't that awful to shock you like that with "the old order changeth"—worrying you about books, etc. But it won't be so very terrifying & we'll figure out something. Got lots of Mike's & Tim's stuff stored: so someplace will have to be found for that too. I told M. on Mother's Day—she wasn't too surprised—my letters have been these wild cries of joy and astonishment to be home at last. Imagine daring to be disappointed in Robert Graves but I was—ruined & succulent. Reminds me: there's a Succulent & Hiking Society here. What *isn't* here—except—but no, everything.

Love, A.

*Ardyth's address changed to 207 East 37th, Room 505.*

LETTER; DECEMBER 24, 1963

12/24/63

Dearest Freddy,

I know you are *relieved* that I didn't send you a card & a present because then you would have had to scurry around & find *me* one. Unless frankly, my dear, to paraphrase what the man said, not now giving a damn you'd just have ignored it. And will this. But don't, baby. I'd feel *so* bad. Because all that happened was, I was drug off by the hair like poor Persephone to toil in the nether regions & then, after getting sprung, waited like a fool for news to send. [. . .] As all continues silence, though—except that the revision was okay—& assuming I'm not going to score many Brownie points on the new book, Thataway, a play called The Queen of Utah & the completely rewritten Nevada novel, here I am finally writing—to somebody maybe by now who couldn't care less.... And I hope not for you are still my baby bee & I am still "the oldest & must know better."

Have been in a hotel on the edge of the Village & must say Michael did himself proud to find it for me. Was just perfect for work & for some unknown reason (maybe the thick walls) nobody even complained when I typed late at night though I was always holding my breath. It's not expensive & here's where I'd live only that women have this unfortunate instinct to cook, scrub floors, etc.—so I've got my eye on an apt., also in this neighborhood & hope to move by the first week in Feb. Then I'm going to tell the New Yorkers I know I'm here & ask *them* not to be mad at me (but I'm not going to say I was here not Portland all the time). Seems like that's all I'm ever doing—apologizing for being myself & a nut, which naturally I can't help, or I would.

[. . .]

Well, I'm beginning to eye the 2nd hand stores & am also finding out where the best bookstores are. . . . And the town's as great as it was, or greater. Of course the North Wind doth blow & we shall have (more) snow & what will the robyn do then poor thing? but one can be so cozy it surely must be a sin.

I felt sorry not to go through the book-burning *with* anybody (except Ruby's Wesley who helped start the fire, then had chores to do) & have our gay Walpurgis night, but doing it in one of the home fields, over the old gully, down by the grape patch, I realized I'd have about burst, trying to be merry & hostessy—for it was a sad, sad thing—my tears nearly put out the fire—all those days & years, Egon's & mine, all our hopes & schemes—well, you can imagine what I was thinking while the fire burned. Now I know why the devil always carries a pitch-fork. It was a hard job (physically) & took more than an hour of assiduous tending. And big ashes blew about as big as big black leaves off some mournful tree & when it was all over it just looked like a place where some hoboes had gathered to warm themselves & make some coffee & then move on & I guess that's all the whole thing really was from beginning to end.

Are you still frowsting on Sunday? And is there still peanut butter for tea?

I don't say anything about Kennedy's death except that my heart nearly broke in two as I suppose yours did too.

Is there any book I *have* to read?

And what's your favorite record now?

Don't know whether I'll dare get a TV when I start house-keeping; get a lot more done without it if you're a natural born lotus-eater.

Can you imagine—I haven't even seen my agent. (Michael's my courier.) He hasn't read Thataway; but liked the plot, not the way I wrote, The Queen of Utah, and the way I wrote, but not the plot of In Nevada. The worst trouble is, writing isn't the most important thing in life for me—it's only about 4th or 5th & the Goddess won't stand for *that*.

What will you stand for, darling? I'll know when & if I hear from you again.

> As always,
> Ardyth

P.S. Am thinking, Merry Xmas—& how you hate the season to be jolly—

*Ardyth's address was now changing to 230 West 16th St., Apt. 1-A.*

LETTER; JANUARY 29, 1964. Enclosure: a clipping torn ("no scissors handy," Ardyth wrote at the top) from the *New York Times* of Jan. 26, 1964, "2 Betting Rooms in 'Village' Shut"; the article describes the arrest of a "well-known 'Village' bookie" — Gaetano Musto, also known as Tommy the Priest.

1/29/64

Dearest Freddy—

Did you ever read that short story about the cat sunning itself in the window & how the mistress had no more idea what that cat had gone through than fly to the moon? Well, apparently it was the same with your letter which was just slipped under Michael's door *yesterday*—maybe from Tommy the Priest's own pocket. And in another week Michael & Judy would have moved to Weehawken. Not because of fright or danger—living where they did safeguarded them, like being in the eye of the storm. And I am moving *today* to my right home which is Apt. 1-A, 230 West 16th, N. Y. so can't answer yr. letter properly till later—your darling New Year's Day letter—& all

this time you were thinking it was pearls cast before swine—
Got *so* much to tell you & will tell you, too. Who BUT you? 'One
may be pardoned, yes I know one may, for
    love undying—'
    Ardyth

TELEGRAM; FEBRUARY 13, 1964

ROSES VIOLETS SUGAR AND WHO SHOULD WANNA
HOLD YOUR HAND ON VALENTINES DAY BUT
    ARDYTH

POSTCARD; APRIL 1, 1964

                    4/1/64
C.B.S. flying witch over kicking & screaming (she hates to fly)
April 5th. Have to meet at Idlewild. TV program April 8th—
watch for it. Begs me to go to everything, stay with her, hold her
hand. Wish you were here to do the same—not for her—me—
    Love, A.

POSTCARD; APRIL 3, 1964

                    4/3/64
(So proud I can write the date like that. Learning took only 4
decades.)
    Today when the book came & just as I was unwrapping it a
cable from Sorceress saying Arriving Monday 1435 hours flight
BA505 love Sybil—& promises tonight & tomorrow night so 4
million things to do, I sat right down, turned pages, read & was
& am crying, got my goat. Isn't she *something*.
P.S. What the heck time is 1435 hours? Love & kisses.

LETTER; JULY 26, 1964

                    Sunday
Freddy dear,
    Well, sir, you sent me such a cute birthday card with just the
real right thing written on it, which you used to say, and I
wonder if you still do? You would be surprised to know that

isolated as you are & in that prison of a P.O., nevertheless somehow you're hipper than even the most hip I have met in hip New York & the Village (it's not all hip), and if you came here, at the hippest party you would fit right in.

Now I am going to reread your letters of— no— no— and answer them. Did I really leave on Sept. 10th? In Nevada & The Queen of Utah got nowhere. Weighty Matters is viewed as a possible money-maker (they always have to think that, I guess) by a beatle haircut editor, John Pope, no relation to Alexander; fussing about illus. now; pub. date still not set. Agent crazy about Thataway; promised to re-write but instead (as when I took off on Good Morning, Young Lady instead of following P.B.'s suggestion to blow up character of little girl in Up Home) started another book so lovely that when I'm making my coffee in the morning, I Only Wanna Be with You is what I'm humming & thinking. 38 pages done, it'll go on forever; working title is: If My Little Dog Barks.

Did I say writing was a 4th or 5th thing? Do I contradict myself? Well, then, I contradict myself.

The fellers have a thing going here, speak to any woman or girl, any age, coming down the street alone, figure that out of a hundred maybe one will respond, but don't stop, keep on walking; hello, baby—where's the party tonight?—where are you going?—helLO, are you THERE? (Eng. accent, old British movies)—and the one I like best—*later for you, baby*.

Later for me came homesickness only about 2 weeks ago. For the first time the alien corn got a little too high. Well, it's awfully hot here, or was. My burglar alarm I can't put on at night without hermetically sealing doors & windows, and the problem is, shall I be drawn & quartered by a homicidal maniac or melt away into a pool of butter like Little Black Sambo's tagger, as Timmy used to say. If I forget to turn it off in the morning before I open the door to the mailman or somebody it just about blasts us out into the street. The mailman has this nervous tic. Then, I was never one that wanted to get promoted, though of course I was always glad after it happened, that I was in the 4th instead of the 3rd like a big girl—and so I am now—

glad— But about 2 wks. ago, I don't know just what happened, but I thought of giving up.

One thing I'm hooked on—the subways—and never take that old A train without wanting to die of joy.

And like today, for instance. At 5 p.m. Michael & I are going to hear a talk about her career by Geraldine Page, then to the Stage delicatessen across from the Americana for dinner where you might see anybody & get insanely good food. Then to the 55th St. Theatre to see THE one & only BEAUTY & THE BEAST. (Judy is up in Montreal dancing in a chorus for 3 wks.) The other day, caught in the Shriner's parade, who should I see only an arm's length away in a taxi but *Michael Rennie*. And Freddy dear, I don't know how they do it but in person they are PERFECT like they just rose up out of Forest Lawn.

I like my apt. though it's on the street; 4 small rooms, high ceilings, tile bath very Gemutlichkeit (sp.), have a hard time getting out. Bookcases built by 2 Calabrians, whole thing painted white by a Spaniard; blind landlord, blinded May, 1936, in Spain; officer in the American forces, Abraham Lincoln brigade; painted by Moses Soyer *before*, so you can see the blue eyes that the hand grenade exploded. Exactly at noon. Married to a blind girl, he about 52, she about 40; married 3 yrs., 2 babies, great big buggy with side curtains & everything parked outside *my* door because I've got the 1st apt. but I don't mind.

I like Jack Jones, too, especially that song that first you pity, then embrace, *On the First Night of the Full Moon* that for some unknown reason when I'm washing dishes or putting up my hair makes me start blinking & swallowing. Haven't got a good radio, just Mother's little transistor, no phonograph & TV & so going right back into the dark ages. Puerto Rican boys have a fad here, go around with a little transistor slung on one hip like a pistol.

Gee, those lines were so wonderful anent the assassination; I know & know them not. I was one of the rumdums who EXULTED when the smirking killer was hit but now realize nothing could have been worse.

You say please destroy your letter but ain't I glad I didn't. And won't, so there. And may even sue you for saying I'm your one best creature & then not grappling me to you with hoops of steel so I couldn't get promoted. And now here's the Feb. letter wit' the clippings, where you were so annoyed wit' After the Fall. Well, who wasn't, I wonder. As everyone is with Harlow, which of course you have? If I'm not mistaken, Barbara Loden was the girl in She Loves Me, to go back to After the Fall again. I understand Arthur Miller & that German wife I unreasonably detest, looks, actions, being a skier, photographer & smart-aleck, capable, snippy, everything Marilyn wasn't who knew that all there was, was love, lives up on 23rd in that famous old hotel up there 7 blocks away. I've got a two-year lease on this place—when the time is up, if Weighty Matters or If My Little Dog Barks or something does good, and if the Lord is willing & the crick don't rise, why, first, I'm coming home for a long visit—no, I'll be home before that—(On the 1st night, on *every* first night of the full moon)—and then I'm going to move into the Dakota, the oldest, poshest & most glamorous apt. house in the entire Apple, with sentries out in front like in Graustark in little pointed kiosks. It's catching before hanging though—long waiting list, cooperative, etc. etc.—I'll have to do VERY good. When you come we'll walk past there & you'll see why I'm nearly out of my mind about it. But then, I am about so many things. Or just, period.

Did you look up Anzia Yezierska? Damnedest old woman I ever met [. . .]. Her daughter Louise got married June 12—as old as John Dewey's daughter would be, which you know she is, to a groom 38. Very cute couple, though; he's a prof. of physics at Purdue. Witch coming back next month, as mad as the winds. Thinking you might get a kick out of them, am enclosing a couple of her letters. You don't have to send them back. The Prof. Westbrook she's talking about lives in Troy, N.Y., Eng. Prof., young friend of Anzia's (young in comparison with her), just met him a few weeks ago—Teach Me Tonight was always my favorite song; he quotes & I know what he's quoting (sometimes); nearly as cute & witty as you are. But not quite.

Oh, Freddy, *is* it true that "whatever is lost like a you or a me / It's always ourselves we find in the sea"? (My butcher gave me a pike the other day that he caught on his vacation. Did you ever see one? Face just like Donald Duck.) But maybe we aren't lost—

Later—

Ardyth

Didn't get mailed yesterday. Geraldine Page very ticky tacky— long straggly bleached hair, shiny nose, dowdy navy blue sack dress; half hr. late; so shy I couldn't believe it—like it was me— and they've got to have those great writers. But aff. and nice & with people in the audience asking questions & helping her along she did fine. Wept at ovation, very nervous. And about Beauty & the Beast—a movie has its luck with one too, like a book—& we had the dreadful misfortune to see Orpheus first. Wish we had seen him coming. That Cocteau was really a glug.

# *Notes*

---

*Letters cited are from a private family collection.*

page 1: "a bereft widow": Ardyth's husband, Egon Victor Ullman, died suddenly on February 2, 1962.

page 1: "what I got from the books": Ardyth published five novels between 1949 and 1956, two of them Literary Guild book-of-the-month selections (*The Peaceable Kingdom* for December 1949 and *Good Morning, Young Lady* for May 1953), which assured substantial sales. Houghton Mifflin published four of her books, and Victor Gollancz published one (*The Spur*).

page 2: "so I could write again like a professional author": Sybil's letters to Ardyth show that Ardyth must have also asked her to help Ardyth's stepsister, Ruby Muller, who had cancer. In a letter of June 26, 1964, from Bashley, England, Sybil mentions that she was beginning to see Ruby's "aura" and assures Ardyth that she is "concentrating for all I am worth." (Ruby died August 13, 1964.)

page 3: "By that time Sybil and I were quite well acquainted": The earliest surviving letter of Sybil to Ardyth is dated June 26, 1964, and addressed to Ardyth at 230 West 16th Street, New York. Sybil opened the letter with "My dear Ardyth." Ardyth had arrived in New York in early 1963 and moved to the 16th Street address on January 29, 1964 (see p. 52).

page 4: "tall women": Ardyth notes in her memoir of her life with her husband that she was "five feet, ten inches tall" (*Bodies Adjacent: Ardyth's Memoir & Egon's Journal* [Sunnycroft Books, 2023], p. 37).

page 6: "Her name was Anzia Yezierska": In a biography of Anzia, her daughter, Louise Levitas Henriksen, describes how her mother had

> turned to a woman crossing at the same time to ask for help, because the sun's glare blinded her. This was Ardyth Ullman, with whom Anzia developed an extraordinary understanding. [. . .] Ullman was middle-aged, perceptive, a sensitive fellow writer who, from that first moment on the street, appreciated Anzia's rebellious, icon-smashing spirit. Volunteering help, which Anzia readily accepted, she was at once drawn into a crisis: Anzia had to undergo surgery promptly to remove a cataract in her right eye; the vision in her left had just been destroyed by a hemorrhage. She planned to enter the hospital without bothering Louise, and insisted that the medical insurance policy [. . .] would cover the costs. But it didn't. Ullman, who took her to the hospital, wrote a check behind her back for the several hundred dollars the hospital asked before admitting Anzia and then wrote Louise.

Anzia came to rely on Ardyth and became "fearful that some bolt from heaven might end this unusual devotion" (Louise Levitas Henriksen, *Anzia Yezierska: A Writer's Life* [Rutgers University Press, 1988], p. 290).

page 9: "Gollancz published some of my books": The Victor Gollancz publishing company brought out Ardyth's book *The Spur* in 1951; and an edition of *Up Home* in 1956 (first published by Houghton Mifflin in 1955).

page 10: "she introduced me to Louise": According to the *Wilmington Morning News* of April 11, 1964 (p. 10), this was Mrs. Louise Hampton, an "apprentice" witch.

page 10: "This was Tuesday": The episode of *To Tell the Truth* in which Sybil Leek appeared aired on Monday, April 13, 1964, but presumably it was taped earlier, on Wednesday the eighth. Ardyth's recollection here that Sybil arrived on a Tuesday conflicts with the postcards Ardyth wrote to her Portland literary friend Frederic "Freddy" Jacobson on April 1 and 3, 1964 (see p. 53).

page 13: "Gasner's Restaurant": Ardyth's manuscript had "the Stork Club," but either her informant or Ardyth herself apparently confused the club with Gasner's Restaurant in Manhattan, another establishment frequented by prominent people. Robert Raven's mother-in-law, Minnie Gasner, ran the restaurant, which was "a landmark dining spot. [. . .] every mayor of New York City came by, all the governors, New York's U.S. senators, a hundred congressmen, lawyers, their clients—and just plain people" (Edward O'Neill, City Hall column, New York *Daily News*, July 23, 1973, p. 4).

page 14: "She was born blind, I guess": Robert Raven's wife, Cele Gasner Raven, was blinded in a household accident at age five (Hackensack, N.J., *Record*, June 3, 1982, p. B1).

page 14: "got injured by grenades": Ardyth's manuscript had "stepped on a land mine," but in fact Raven's injuries in the Spanish Civil War of 1936–39 were caused by grenades. (See Raven's biography in the Abraham Lincoln Brigade Archives, at https://alba-valb.org/volunteers/robert-joseph-raven.)

Coincidentally, Raven and other veterans of the Abraham Lincoln Brigade held a demonstration at the Spanish pavilion at the World's Fair in New York City on July 18, 1964—the same summer that Ardyth visited the fair with her husband's cousin (see p. 40). Raven handed a petition to the pavilion's manager appealing to the Spanish authorities to release all political prisoners (Robert Alden, "Veterans of the Lincoln Brigade Demonstrate at Spanish Pavilion," *New York Times*, July 19, 1964, p. 64).

The character Gene Abeloff in Ardyth's novel *Variation West* (published in 2014) is based partly on Robert Raven.

page 15: "She never went back home": Sybil did return to England for a short time before coming back to the United States to live. She wrote to Ardyth on June 26, 1964, from Bashley, England; another letter followed on July 8, from the same address; and in a letter to Freddy of July 26, 1964, Ardyth wrote, "Witch coming back next month, as mad as the winds" (see p. 56).

page 15: "a wonderful black dress": In an interview of April 12, 2012, Michael remembered that the dress was purple.

page 15: "she seemed to have forgotten. . . . how I had met her . . . at the JFK airport": Sybil apparently didn't forget; in a letter of September 15, 1967, from Dublin, she wrote to Ardyth: "You were the first real person I knew (or did not know?) in America & when you became a shadow yourself with all the elements of rejection in your removal from New York, I think I lost a lot of faith in humanity."

page 16: "Years ago, I was particularly upset . . .": This quotation can be found on page 51 of the 1975 Bantam edition of *Reincarnation: The Second Chance*.

page 17: "At first we kept in touch": Two letters from Sybil to Ardyth from the summer of 1964 have survived (see note to p. 15, above). On June 26, Sybil mentioned her efforts in behalf of Ardyth's ill stepsister, responded extensively to Ardyth's diet "program" for her (Sybil), and commented on closing her antique shop in England before her return to America: "Packed up the shop, finished there on Wednesday and strangely enough no regrets."

Sybil wrote to Ardyth at least eleven more times, between January 1967 and May 1968, after a chance meeting with Ardyth's niece in Louisville while Sybil was on a lecture tour ("I hate to lose touch with people whom I have once appreciated as a friend," she wrote on January 27). Her warm regard for Ardyth in subsequent letters was evident: she addressed her as "My dearest Ardyth" or even "Dearest Momma-Aunt," and would close with "All my love to you" or "This comes to you with more love than perhaps you will realise." She praised Ardyth's talent ("If I had your brains I'd be God"); entreated her repeatedly to continue writing books and send manuscripts for Sybil to read; offered to act as her agent with publishers; invited her several times to visit in Los Angeles and later Florida (apparently Ardyth never did); and told her that she (Sybil) and her two sons were "practically your adopted family."

Ardyth did send Sybil several of her manuscripts; Sybil sent back comments on them, but an author-agent relationship apparently never materialized. Still, Sybil—herself a prolific and successful author—appreciated Ardyth's writing talent. On March 23, 1967, she wrote: "I still get mad about your writing though,..you simply do not take the politics of writing seriously enough. There you are,..with a brain as big as the Universe, a talent for beautiful phrases & you do not pull out all stops to go sailing along."

page 17: "gave up witchcraft and being a witch": Sybil's answer to Ardyth in a letter of May 13, 1968, indicates that she still considered herself a witch: "Have I given up witchcraft,..perish the thought, it is with me all the time but I revolt against the extrovertness which is demanded by the American public. Extrovert though I am,..somehow the better things of life such as a religion or a philosophy for life are the secret parts which it seems indecent to parade in public."

Ardyth herself, although from a Mormon family, did not subscribe to any particular religious or spiritual beliefs. However, she seems to have been intrigued by the possibility of supernatural elements at work in the world.

page 17: "extreme examples of intolerance . . .": See page 52 of *Reincarnation* (Bantam, 1975).

page 18: "a nice young English professor": This was James Seymour Westbrook Jr., who received his master's and Ph.D. degrees from Columbia University and in 1964 was an associate professor of English at Rensselaer Polytechnic Institute in Troy, New York ("Two RPI Professors Get Degrees," *The Times-Record* [Troy, N.Y.], June 22, 1964, p. 15). Diana Westbrook, James Westbrook's daughter, confirmed in a phone interview of November 25, 2023, that her father was interested in Anzia's work and visited her; and although he did not write a book about her, he may have been helping her write some autobiographical material.

page 18: "a tongue that ran like a squirrel in the park": This is apparently a reference to "How She Resolved to Act," a sonnet by Merrill Moore, whose final line is "And her tongue raced like a squirrel in the park."

page 19: "One of her novels . . . live in Hollywood": This passage contains some remarks that are contradicted by other sources, including Anzia's daughter's biography of her mother (Levitas Henriksen, *Anzia Yezierska*). Possibly Ardyth misunderstood what Anzia told her, or misremembered it when she wrote this memoir thirty-seven years later; but it's also possible that what Anzia told Ardyth didn't reflect the actual facts of her life. As Levitas Henriksen wrote of her mother: "Whenever she talked about herself, to interviewers or even to intimates, she had a way of rearranging or inventing the facts to suit her current feelings" (pp. 1–2). As one example of the unreliability of Ardyth's passage, the woman who married Milton Ager, composer of "Happy Days Are Here Again," was not Anzia's sister but her niece, the film critic Cecelia (Rubenstein) Ager (p. 199).

page 19: "and had, so she told me, a daughter by him": The father of Anzia's daughter (Louise) was her second husband, Arnold Levitas. Although Anzia did have a relationship with John Dewey, it did not start until five years after Louise's birth (*Anzia*, pp. 56, 85).

page 19: "who had never married herself": Anzia married the lawyer Jacob Gordon in 1910 but applied for an annulment the following day. She married Arnold Levitas, a teacher, in a religious ceremony in 1911 (*Anzia*, pp. 37, 44–45).

page 20: "inviting her to come to Princeton": Anzia had just had cataract surgery, and her daughter had arranged for her "to convalesce at her fiancé's apartment on the campus of the Institute for Advanced Study in Princeton" (*Anzia*, p. 290).

page 20: "She invited me, too": During Anzia's stay in Princeton, Ardyth "made the trip from New York City several times a week, bringing flowers and cake; she telephoned Anzia daily. [. . .] Ullman was her chief comfort during the two-week period of rigid, enforced idleness" (*Anzia*, p. 290).

page 20: "well, I don't have to tell you": Ardyth is referring to the Princeton "Dinky," the train that is "a unique symbol of Princeton University that has grown over time to emblemize the university. It is mentioned in F. Scott Fitzgerald's *This Side of Paradise*" ("Princeton Branch," Wikipedia, accessed Nov. 2, 2023).

page 20: "a Louise somebody": This was, of course, Anzia's daughter, Louise Levitas Henriksen.

page 21: "and they took it!": The story about the bird, titled "The Open Cage," was not in fact published until 1979, in *The Open Cage: An Anzia Yezierska Collection* (Persea Books). Anzia did publish a different story, called "A Window Full of Sky," in *The Reporter* magazine of July 2, 1964 (not *The New Republic*). In a letter to Anzia's niece Cecelia Ager from around that time, Ardyth refers to "the publication of that little story in the *Reporter*" that had "restored her faith in herself and her gifts" (quoted in *Anzia*, p. 291).

page 21: "I didn't see Anzia too much after that": Anzia's daughter explains how the two women's relationship fell apart:

> Ardyth Ullman's continuing help began to seem less valuable to Anzia after she recovered from the [eye] surgery. Telephoning more frequently, Anzia became dissatisfied when Ullman failed to respond as promptly as she once had. And if Ullman, answering one of Anzia's emergency-distress calls, for example, did take a pair of custom-made shoes back to the shoemaker and could not get Anzia's money back, that was a black mark against her in Anzia's mind; and she dispatched someone else on the same fruitless errand. "She's got everybody working and all kinds of things going for her, as you know," Ullman wrote to Louise, "bureaus, services, Social Security departments . . . private people, old and young. . . . One reason why she lowered the boom on me was [that] I had the temerity to . . . tease her . . . and say she was like Napoleon up there in that room of hers . . . deploying her troops."
>
> Now cold and resentful, Anzia telephoned Ullman one day to say she was canceling their appointment, she didn't want to see Ullman again. "You're false—false," she told her over the phone. "I knew it was too good to be true, pretending to be Lady Bountiful!" (*Anzia*, p. 292)

Another account is given in Bettina Berch, *From Hester Street to Hollywood: The Life and Work of Anzia Yezierska* (New York: Sefer International, 2009), p. 211: "Later that year [1964], Ardyth wrote Louise and described how Yezierska had given her a major tongue-lashing, a 'torrent of vituperation'; apparently Ardyth had called Yezierska 'darling,' a term that seemed to enrage her. But later that night, Yezierska called Ardyth and told her she'd be busy with new speaking engagements and didn't think she'd have much time to see her."

page 25: "Miss Desfossés": Born around 1904, Beatrice Desfossés was a concert singer from Montreal who had studied and performed in Europe and New York. In the 1930s she became a speech consultant and coach in New York City, giving private lessons and also teaching at Finch Junior College in Manhattan. In 1947 she published a book, *Your Voice and Your Speech: Self-Training for Better Speaking*. The Montreal *Gazette* described Miss Desfossés as "tall and slender, blonde and with deep violet eyes" and possessing a "golden voice," with a "personality of rare charm" (Sept. 9, 1930, p. 9).

page 28: "Sanders—that was my escort's name": Ardyth never mentions Sanders's full name, but there are clues in a letter she wrote in about 1986 to her friend Freddy Jacobson that this was the poet Sanders Russell (1913–1982), associated with Robert Duncan, with whom he founded the poetry magazine *Experimental Review* in 1940:

> The batch of books Arlyn brought just about floored me. A thousand thanks. Where did you ever find the Young Robert Duncan. The minute Arlyn & Billy left I made more coffee & curdled [*sic*] up on the couch to look up every mention of Sanders, then sat bemused. I was glad to find out he died—I mean, what happened to him, as for the past few Xmases I haven't heard from him. You know I never knew he had met all those people—Kenneth Patchen, Pauline Kael, Anais Nin etc. or I'd have been like that woman in Plaza Suite.

We had a funny friendship, hardly talked at
all. Certainly not about literary stuff, except he'd
be taken with a book like Aldous Huxley's wife's
about mind sets etc. & wouldn't talk about
anything else. Mostly we ran around looking at
things he would point out to me, buildings, the
cul de sac where E. E. Cummings had lived,
Edward Sheldon's windows, Coney Island dead
and deserted on a winter night with the snow
coming down in big flakes, the ocean out there
like—nothing, kind of a scalloped edge to the
night.

[. . .] Looking back I'm surprised at him
wanting to be friends with me, me being a girl
(aged 50) & everything, but he became quite a
buddy. [. . .]

Of course I babied him, had him for lots of
meals & when we were out I paid for everything—not great expenditures just subway
tokens & cheap restaurants like the automat. He
never talked about any of the stuff in this book
(so far as I can tell by just a quick look). How he
did need someone to take care of him! so stiff-
necked in the old biblical sense, prickly, bitchy,
wouldn't let anybody come too close but yet he
did let me come close in a way. The tragedy of
Sanders was not that he was a poet but that he
was always just living the life. Sibling rivalry
was behind it (his brother could really write).
His stuff was awful, like written by a computer
with cloth ears. [. . .]

Thank you for these books. Poor Sanders. He
looks beautiful in that picture when he lived in
Woodstock, like a real poet. And noble and sad
in the other picture "shortly before his death." I
wonder what he died of? You know he nearly
got murdered one time—stabbed.

(From Robert Duncan's biography at Poets.org: "In 1938, after two years at University of California, Berkeley, Duncan moved to New York and became involved in the downtown literary coterie that had sprung up around Anaïs Nin. [. . .] During this time, Duncan launched the *Experimental Review* with Sanders Russell; Duncan and Russell published the work of Henry Miller, Anaïs Nin, Kenneth Patchen, Lawrence Durrell, and other writers in their circle.")

page 31: "Grandpa was arrested": Ardyth's maternal grandfather, Emil Oscar Olsen, married Matilda Sophia Larsen in 1873 and then, six years later, married Ardyth's grandmother, Anna Matilda Johnson. Ardyth's cousin William Scott Fisher explains in his *History of Our Olsen Family Ancestors* (1989): "As Emil was going about the task of building up his tailoring business [in Salt Lake City], United States Federal agents were monitoring his movements and documenting the facts surrounding his and other polygamous marriages. The surveillance of the Olsens began on May 1, 1883, and culminated with his arrest on charges of 'illegal cohabitation' around 6 pm on the evening of Friday, April 17, 1885 at his tailor shop. The charge was made under the authority of the Edmunds Law of 1882, which had made polygamy a crime. The agents had no doubt observed the addition of Laura Elise Olsen to Emil and Anna's family on April 12, 1884, and were aware of the impending birth of another child by Matilda. [. . .] Emil was tried and found guilty on Saturday, October 3, 1885. He was sentenced to six months in prison and a fine of $300 on Tuesday, October 13, 1885. The horse-drawn carriage took him off to the Utah Territorial Penitentiary that same day."

page 33: "Ernesto and Adele . . . got acquainted with certain of these itinerant performers": The classical pianist and conductor Daniel Barenboim wrote in 2002:

> In the 1940s Buenos Aires was a musical centre.
> [. . .] Arturo Toscanini came, and Wilhelm Furt-
> wängler, the young Herbert von Karajan, and

Richard Strauss before that. Wilhelm Backhaus, Walter Gieseking, Artur Rubinstein, Erich Kleiber and Claudio Arrau also spent a lot of time there. [. . .]

All the musicians in Buenos Aires, and anybody who was on tour in Argentina, went to No. 1257 Talcahuano, the house of the Austrian-Jewish family of Ernesto Rosenthal, where chamber music was played on Friday evenings. (Rosenthal himself was an amateur violinist.) I had two encounters there that greatly influenced me. One was with Sergiu Celibidache, for whom I played when I was seven or eight. [. . .] The other important encounter I had at Rosenthal's home was with Igor Markevich, the Russian conductor and composer. [. . .] At the Rosenthals' chamber music evenings I would play for anybody who was willing to listen, and people were always curious to hear what a seven-year-old could do (*A Life in Music* [New York: Arcade Publishing, 2002], pp. 3–5).

page 33: "Adele got sick": Egon wrote in his journal on October 15, 1955: "My cousin Ernesto Rosenthal from Buenos Aires writes me quite regularly, and long letters. Lately there was more news from him, first because Olly, his wife, had to have an eye removed in Vienna because of a tumor, and then because Peron and the Peronistas have been overthrown and the Rosenthals are quite excited about it" (*Bodies Adjacent*, p. 135). Egon noted on April 3, 1956, that "Olly Rosenthal died of sarcomatosis and I have been comforting Ernesto across 5,000 miles to Buenos Aires" (p. 139).

page 33: "six or seven stair-step Duncans": Isadora had only three siblings; possibly Ardyth was thinking of other groups of young people who danced with Isadora or under her instruction.

page 34: "one of the boys, Raymond": Ardyth's manuscript had "the youngest boy, Laurence," and she continued to refer to him as Laurence throughout. However, this was surely Raymond Duncan; there was no Laurence in the family.

page 35: "The free lecture didn't last long": It's uncertain when this "lecture" might have occurred, but Raymond Duncan was scheduled to present a one-man "spontaneous" play called *Ship Ahoy* at Carnegie Hall on November 28, 1964. He had arrived in New York on October 28 by ship, "on his perennial Paris to New York run" ("Art Notes," *New York Times*, November 15, 1964, p. 24X).

page 39: "my heart just almost burst": Ardyth had a strong interest in Lincoln and his assassination. Her 1951 book *The Spur* is a fictionalized but well researched account of the last days of John Wilkes Booth. Ardyth wrote to her mother in April 1944 after she and Egon, who was stationed on the East Coast with the Army at the time, had been in Washington, D.C.: "What thrilled me most in Washington was, of course, the old Ford's Theatre where Lincoln was shot and the little house across the way where they carried him to die and where Seward said as they closed his eyes 'Now he belongs to the ages.' Everything's just as it was then." On May 2, 1948, Egon wrote in his journal: "Sometimes at night she is reading about Lincoln's assassination, which holds an everlasting fascination for her. I had to take the book away from her and suggested she not read it at night because she gets so terribly excited about it that she cannot go to sleep" (*Bodies Adjacent*, pp. 65–66).

page 42: "And that will be the best": The last stanza of A. E. Housman's poem "A Shropshire Lad VII" reads:

> *Lie down, lie down, young yeoman;*
> *The sun moves always west;*
> *The road one treads to labour*
> *Will lead one home to rest,*
> *And that will be the best.*

page 44: "And our Empress ate an entire sixteen-course dinner!": This is a sarcastic comment; Empress Elisabeth of Austria was obsessed with dieting and remaining thin. The only surviving chapter of the history of dieting that Ardyth wrote, in probably the 1960s, was about the empress.

page 48: "on March 30th": Presumably Ardyth meant May 30, since she refers to Mother's Day two sentences later. Mother's Day was on May 12 in 1963.

page 48: "I haven't told Marion either": Marion was Ardyth's younger sister.

page 50: "Mike's & Tim's stuff": These were Ardyth's nephews.

page 51: "Ruby's Wesley": Wesley Muller was the second husband of Ardyth's stepsister, Ruby (Parker Olsen) Muller. Ruby and Wesley resided in the North Albany home where Ardyth lived from age 11 to age 23.

page 52: "maybe from Tommy the Priest's own pocket": As Ardyth mentions in the memoir, Michael and Judy lived on MacDougal Street; they were at the same address as the gambling establishment.

page 54: "that prison of a P.O.": Freddy worked for the post office.

page 54: "Weighty Matters": This was probably the history of dieting that Ardyth wrote, of which only one full and one partial chapter survive.

page 54: "P.B.'s suggestion": Paul Brooks was Ardyth's editor at Houghton Mifflin for her earlier novels.

page 55: "painted by Moses Soyer *before*": The portrait is dated 1939 and was therefore painted *after* Robert Raven was blinded (which happened in 1937, not 1936). See note to p. 14.

page 56: "John Dewey's daughter": See note to p. 19.

page 56: "a prof. of physics": Louise's husband, Melvin Henriksen, was a professor of mathematics.

pages 56–57: "The Prof. Westbrook she's talking about": See note to p. 18.

# Index of Names

Printed in the USA
CPSIA information can be obtained
at www.ICGtesting.com
LVHW072356101124
796145LV00010B/33

* 9 7 8 0 9 9 0 4 3 2 0 4 3 *